RMS
LUSITANIA
IT WASN'T & IT DIDN'T

Dr Michael Martin

RMS
LUSITANIA
IT WASN'T & IT DIDN'T

MICHAEL MARTIN

First published 2014, reprinted 2015

The History Press Ireland
50 City Quay
Dublin 2
www.thehistorypress.ie

British Library Cataloguing in Publication Data.
A catalogue record for this book is available from the British Library.

ISBN 978 1 84588 854 1

Typesetting and origination by The History Press
Printed and bound by TJ International Ltd, Padstow Cornwall.

Contents

Acknowledgements

In finishing a book many authors feel that there is much more that could have been written, that particular areas could have been expanded upon or given more detailed explanations. There can be a deep-felt reluctance to 'let it go', punctuated with an insatiable desire to get back into it and begin to update, amend and rewrite all over again. On the other hand the people closest to them are often relieved that the project is finally done. In the writing of a book the author will be motivated and driven to put in the late nights, exhaustive research and lengthy discussions but family and friends, who get no immediate benefit, are the ones who are the background and sometimes frontline support without whom the book would never see the light of day. In this regard there are numerous people I would like to acknowledge. Heartfelt thanks to my wife Geraldine and sons Gary Lee and Ken who offered unconditional encouragement throughout all phases of concept, research, writing and delivery; my nephew Aaron Gaynor (imbued with the patience of Joab), who forensically examined the manuscript and made corrections and offered suggestions that undoubtedly added value to the text; Joan Brennan who oversaw all the requirements of the day job in running a busy office for me in my absence; the many authors and researchers whose work I consulted in the course of writing this book; the staff at the Boole Library of University

College Cork; the curator, Heather Bird, and staff of Cobh Museum. Eoin McGarry for sharing his insight into the actuality of the wreck of the ship and its physical legacy; Paddy O'Sullivan and his unwavering encouragement for all things *Lusitania*; the military veteran's organisation of Grand Cayman and in particular Gerry and Ali who orchestrated my visit to speak about the *Lusitania* there; my former colleagues of the Irish Navy who deal on a daily basis with all the vagaries of the Eastern Atlantic that surrounds Ireland; Marcus Connaughton, author, broadcaster, producer and presenter of the *Seascapes Maritime* programme on Irish National Radio; Jim Halligan and fellow members of The Molgoggers Sea Shanty and Maritime Song Group who continue to offer a healthy diversion for mind and spirit when embroiled in the concentration of daily writing; finally to Eamon and Elizabeth Martin whom I have no doubt are proudly looking on from further afield.

Introduction

The Royal Mail Steamship RMS *Lusitania* was torpedoed and sunk by a German submarine on 7 May 1915. Twelve hundred innocent civilians lost their lives that day and became another statistic of what became known as the Great War. The fact that this was a civilian ship and was populated by non-combatants imparted the understandable impression that this action plumbed new depths of inhumanity. Unfortunately, there was nothing new about the slaughter of innocents. Such an event in peacetime would cause consternation around the globe among all peoples. Yet there were some in 1915 that perceived the attack as legitimate. There were some who believed it was justified. Their beliefs arose as a consequence of them being 'at war', the wording that gives latitude for unspeakable acts.

The term 'war' embodies a great diversity of events and occurrences that always mean different things to different people. It is multifaceted, frequently reflecting division and conflict but also political intrigue, deeply held cultural aspirations, greed, cruelty, loss, human tragedy and almost always unspeakable terror for those who are at the receiving end of the mechanics of war. There can be heroism, bravery, kind-heartedness or hostility depending on which side of the conflict the perspective is formed. Centuries of mankind often perceived war to be the playing out of good against evil, right against wrong. In addition, war was often thought to be about man against man. In the classic scenario, foes line up opposite each other on a chosen site and engage on a most personal level in fighting and hand-to-hand combat until numbers, exhaustion or skill lead to one side becoming victorious. The development of weaponry and tactics from as early as Greek and Roman times began a process of distancing opponents from each other. The longbow, the crossbow, the musket and the cannon all had the effect of removing combatants from the point of lethal impact.

In simpler times, justification of the slaughter of enemies may have been easier. Protection of land, upholding of rights, consolidation of food sources and the defence of the most basic needs to survive would have compelled people to believe that war was defensive and necessary. As man developed, complicating factors increased inordinately. The acquisition of internal power, religious beliefs or control and political intrigue resulting in shifting of influence became the commonplace. It was also crucial to persuade citizens (on whose behalf war supposedly took place) that offensive actions were justified and the enemy was at fault. The repeated perspective of one side over another, the eternal narrative of right against wrong directed at the people of participating nations was to be shaped by the use of propaganda which often could be justification for defending the indefensible. Simplistic views of an arch-enemy embodying all that is evil can be comforting; however, such logic can also disguise errors of judgement and even neglect on the part of those who purportedly are fighting from the high moral ground. The loss of over 1,200 lives as a result of the sinking of RMS *Lusitania* in May of 1915 may fall into this category.

The outbreak of the First World War was the classic case of the shifting alliances and the balance of power among a small number of elite royalty having consequences of unimaginable proportions. It was also to become the most advanced and hideous mechanisation of the slaughter of millions of lives. Those that were killed in many cases never saw or heard the weapons of destruction that brought about their demise. Those that killed others in the scales of thousands often did little more than press some buttons or adjust some levers.

However, this did not prevent soldiers in the trenches witnessing the obscene destruction of human tissue and bone among those they had just spoken to or served with. The appalling discomfort of trench life was made worse by the persistent presence of the dead in forms and shapes that should never be seen by fellow human beings. The sheer size and scale of army numbers that were going to be involved were monumental. Germany had 2 million men in uniform ready to mobilise.

One army Corps alone (out of a total of forty in the German forces) required 170 railway carriages for officers, 965 for infantry, 2,960 for cavalry, 1,915 for artillery and supply wagons, 6,010 in all, grouped in 140 trains and an equal number again for their supplies.[1]

Millions of young men, women and children were to die between 1914 and 1918 and yet in some places life went on as normal. Business was conducted, relationships blossomed and died, newspapers were written and food was grown and harvested. Sometimes, however, the sanctity of apparent normality was shattered and those that felt physically removed from the battlefield were brought into the epicentre of destruction – often when least expected. Such was the experience of those sailing on one of the world's most luxurious liners in 1915. On a sunny afternoon in a soft Atlantic swell nearing the end of an otherwise pleasant voyage, those on RMS *Lusitania* had the worst aspects of the war brought to bear on them. Like many who perished in the trenches they did not see their silent enemy. Like those who had the misfortune to be on the front, they too heard the deafening report of explosives and within seconds witnessed death and destruction around them. In the small confines of a ship made tiny by the vastness of the ocean, men, women and children grappled for life over death. Most did not succeed. Of more than 1,900 people on board only 762 survived.

How did such an atrocious attack take place? What events led to the taking of the lives of so many innocent non-combatants? Who was responsible? How did the reach of the battlefield extend so far beyond terra firma? What decisions were made and by whom?

Within hours of the sinking a narrative was created, a perspective was advanced. Some acquired solace from the simplistic explanations that were proffered. Others swore vengeance. This was a savage attack on an innocent vessel.

> War waged by her [Germany] was directed not only against military and Naval forces opposed to her, but against innocent non-combatants whenever she can by the aid of her submarines and aerial craft. Nothing transcends this barbarity.[2]

But was the vessel innocent? Later it would be claimed that this atrocity brought America into the war. But did it? For almost a century the story of the loss of RMS *Lusitania* had been neatly categorised by many as an enemy war-crime. Undoubtedly this gave some closure to those who lost loved ones. But do they deserve more? Should we take the perspective that was offered or should we look for other explanations? The inhabitants of the little town of Queenstown (now Cobh) in County Cork, Ireland, were traumatised when they witnessed the consequences of the attack. The Old Church Cemetery near the town was to become the resting place of many of the victims.

Over 1,200 people died that day and while the following work does not purport to answer all queries, it is hoped that it will at least broaden perspectives and lead to the asking of more pertinent, if uncomfortable, questions in seeking to find out what really happened and why on that beautiful afternoon off the south coast of Ireland on 7 May of 1915.

In the aftermath of the sinking of the ship and in the intervening century since there has been much speculation and many theories advanced. The claims and counterclaims have kept scholars and writers busy over the years. Some books concentrated solely on the passengers and their wealth and influence, others have explored the terror of the incident itself. Almost all take one position or another on what happened and a few have tried to unravel the unanswered questions that remain. And there are many unanswered questions. However, adopting or believing a narrative that evolved which fit in then or fits in now with post-war results does not do the matter justice. Conclusions that were reached while the conflict was still in progress are bound to be heavily influenced by the war and people's perspective on it. There have also been conspiracy and other theories that emerged that counter the official conclusions or seek to shed more light on grey areas. The reality is that even if all facts were laid bare, different perspectives, cultures and positions will lead to different conclusions.

The presence of munitions on board is undisputed, the carrying of .303 ammunition was within the rights of the shipping company according to the regulations at the time and one side can argue that nothing illegal was done. On the other hand, as Paddy O'Sullivan points out in his work, were these not bullets that would be fired at German soldiers and citizens once they reached their destination? If so, was the ship that carried them not a legitimate target? Some would argue that it was but there were procedures in the so called 'rules of war' to board such vessels when civilians were present which could have prevented any loss of life but destroyed the offending munitions. However, British merchant sea captains had been ordered to ram submarines whenever they saw them so others will argue it was impossible to approach such vessels. One conspiracy theory has the British Admiralty and Winston Churchill in particular orchestrating the entire incident. This appears to be highly improbable; however, there were certain actions taken and instructions given that are very likely to have increased the loss of life on the ship, some of which can be traced to the Admiralty. These include four areas in particular: the carriage of passengers into danger by the shipping company Cunard, the presence of an explosive cargo on board the ship, the extensive use of 'civilian' vessels in the fight against submarines, and the actions and inaction of HMS *Juno*.

The cause of the second explosion has been the subject of much conjecture and has been exhaustively examined; however, there are other matters that have not been so closely scrutinised. There is also now the added knowledge given to the world by Mr Bemis, the owner of the wreck, who undertook an expedition to the wreck site with *National Geographic* and beamed images of part of the cargo of ammunition into living rooms around the world as recently as 2012.

The story of the sinking of RMS *Lusitania* has continued to be a subject of discussion among historians, interested parties and scholars for almost a century now. New discoveries appear to raise more questions than they answer. In the public mind there seems to be still a prevailing narrative, very simplistic, very black and white: it was a savage attack on an innocent vessel that brought America into the war. Without detracting from the tragedy of the great loss of innocent lives that day, it is my intention in this book not only to show, it wasn't and it didn't, but also to try and put the incident into its proper historical context. The men, women and children who died that day deserve that we continue to ask the questions and not just accept a narrative handed down by officialdom and conveniently wrapped with a bow of simplicity.

Michael Martin, Cobh, 2014

1

Queenstown and the Queenstown Command

Q ueenstown in Cork Harbour, on the south coast of Ireland, was to witness the main consequences of the sinking of RMS *Lusitania*. The town is now, and was then, the largest town on the largest island in Cork Harbour. Not surprisingly it was named Great Island. Its strategic location along the main shipping route between Europe and the Americas had resulted in it becoming a key stopping-off point on trans-Atlantic voyages. From whenever ships began to explore the oceans beyond the Eastern Atlantic seaboard, Cork Harbour had featured as an important station from where fresh produce, crew, water and cargo could be taken on to augment ships' supplies. It was also a busy commercial port in its own right, with a healthy import and export trade, particularly from the city of Cork. The governing body of Britain's Royal Navy, the Admiralty, had charted the entrance and approaches to Cork Harbour from as early as the sixteenth century. Their strategic interest in the harbour heightened in the early nineteenth century when their preferred location of the nearby harbour of Kinsale had become unsuitable as a result of natural silting. In 1825 the Admiralty Victualling station was moved from Kinsale to Haulbowline Island in Cork Harbour. There had been a British military presence there since Elizabethan times and during the Napoleonic wars major fortifications were upgraded at the entrance to the harbour and on Spike Island. This was probably the busiest time for the port in terms of military activity. Later, in the early 1850s British troops were embarked from Queenstown to and from the Crimean War, as they were during the Boer War in South Africa at the end of the 1800s. The Admiralty came to the area first in 1793. A hillside building was used as their headquarters which provided panoramic views of the harbour and its entrance. The jurisdiction of the Queenstown Command stretched all along the south coast of Ireland, which is right in the path of Britain's strategic Western Approaches. Naval vessels of the Royal Navy had come and gone under the command of the Admiralty for many years. However, from the Boer War through to the First World War the strategic importance of Queenstown had somewhat diminished.

Today the town is known as Cobh and it has built up quite a successful tourism industry through its tenuous connections with the RMS *Titanic*. In 1912 Cork harbour was the last port of call of the ship which only stopped there for ninety minutes before making its fateful voyage across the Atlantic before striking the iceberg. The original buildings where passengers stayed and embarked from are still there. The first *Titanic* attraction in Ireland was established in the town in 1998. The author created an historical walking tour called the Titanic Trail which explores these connections. However, the sinking of RMS *Lusitania* was to have a much greater impact on the town than the *Titanic* ever had. The main consequence of the sinking of *Titanic* was shared between two cities in two different countries. The Cunard ship, *Carpathia*, was the first ship on the scene to pick up survivors from the stricken vessel and took them to New York. It was the officialdom of the city that dealt with the repatriation of survivors back to their home countries or final intended destination. New York also established an official enquiry to ascertain the circumstances of the sinking and the world media gathered there to capture the essence of one of the greatest maritime disasters ever. The recovery operation to retrieve the dead bodies from *Titanic*'s sinking was conducted from Halifax in Nova Scotia, Canada. It was the little Canadian port city that had to deal with the identification of remains, the burials and the notification to families of the fate of their loved ones. In this way it can be said that the immediate consequences of *Titanic*'s demise was shared between two cities in two different countries. In the case of sinking of RMS *Lusitania* (which in human terms was not that much different from *Titanic*) the little town of Cobh found itself at the centre of the consequences of the sinking. The rescue operation, involving the deployment and co-ordination of boats, was arranged there. Hundreds of bodies that were recovered from the sea after the sinking were brought there. Arrangements for the burial of those that died were organised in

Cobh as it is today. (© Michael Martin)

Cobh and the grisly job of identifying the bodies of as many people as possible were all to be witnessed by the people and the professions of Cobh. Happily for those that survived their repatriation was organised and many left from the old railway station to set out on a journey back to Great Britain.

Despite the fact that the ship sank closer to other little port towns such as Kinsale and Courtmacsharry, the Admiralty designated Cobh as the place where victims and survivors should be brought soon after the rescue operations had begun. As a result it was the people of Cobh who witnessed most of the trauma and tragedy that followed. Many fishermen from the town engaged themselves in the rescue operation. Some families opened their homes to offer sanctuary for survivors until they could organise their onward travel. People were to see the bodies of men, women and children being brought from the landing pier to the temporary mortuaries that were set up. They witnessed distraught parents looking for missing children, husbands looking for wives, orphans looking for parents. Ninety-four children died on the RMS *Lusitania*, many having been separated from their mothers during the violent destruction and sinking of the ship.

Most survivors accounts' describe both the speed with which the ship sank and the consequential violence with which the life-boats were destroyed against the hull of the vessel or had their human contents thrown into the sea because of their frenzied deployment.

At the time of the sinking in May of 1915, Cobh was at the centre of a busy military and commercial port. Physically the waterfront area was a series of classic Victorian and Georgian frontages. These buildings housed the various retail outlets, shipping companies, consulates, hotels, restaurants, banks, administrative and operational offices. On any day in Cobh one could witness the movement of ships, ferries and yachts crisscrossing to and fro in the expansive waterway. Royal Naval vessels steamed in and out of harbour regularly, anchoring directly in front of the town in a safe and strategic channel known as 'the Roads'. It seemed as soon as they had anchored, their ships boats would be lowered from their sides and continually ply back and forth to other naval ships anchored nearby for a variety of reasons. Ferries operating in the harbour conveyed people to and from Cork city and to many of the small coastal towns around the harbour. Civilians going about their daily business found that ferry routes offered a much faster means of travel than using the road systems. Sometimes a short ferry journey could obviate the need for a lengthy road journey taking hours instead of minutes.

Military launches brought personnel from and between the major military installations comprising of forts and barracks on Haulbowline, Spike Island, Crosshaven and Whitegate. Forts Westmoreland, Camden and Carlisle positioned at these places formed the strategic defence of the entire harbour and its approaches. Despite its former military and maritime importance, Cobh at the beginning of the First World War was quite distant from the main theatre of operations of the Royal Navy.

The newly appointed Admiral Sir John Jellicoe as commander of the grand fleet of the Royal Navy of Great Britain held that the use of the navy centred on four points:

- It was absolutely vital for the navy to ensure the unimpeded use of the seas for British ships, because Britain as an island nation was not self-sufficient.
- In the event of war the navy should bring steady economic pressure on the enemy by denying him the use of the sea.
- The navy should cover the passage and assist any army sent overseas and protect its communication and supplies.
- The navy should prevent the invasion of Great Britain and its dominions by enemy forces.[1]

To give effect to the control of the seas, the Royal Navy were to effectively cut off access to the Atlantic and so other oceans by controlling the North Sea. Twenty-four Dreadnoughts and four battle cruisers were stationed at Scapa Flow and twelve cruisers carried out northern patrols. Eighteen pre-Dreadnoughts and four cruisers were stationed in the south and at Harwich there were two light cruisers, thirty-five destroyers and a submarine flotilla comprising of sixteen E and D class submarines. The Thames estuary, Portsmouth and Devonport were also bases for numerous ships, torpedo boats or submarines of different sizes and classes amounting to over eighty vessels which in the English Channel were augmented by French Naval vessels.

And so the Royal Navy was positioned in heavy concentration to control German access to open oceans and protect the homeland. Other vessels were deployed on the east coast and the entrance to the Irish Sea. In the greater picture Cobh was not seen as such a strategic location for keeping the German surface fleet blockaded. Admiral Coke, who was in charge of Queenstown Command at the time, didn't have a huge number of vessels under his command. However, it would not have been unusual in Cobh to experience all the colour and movement of a bustling seaport: ships' suppliers and chandlers provisioning waiting vessels, uniformed military personnel going about their business, postmasters overseeing delivery and collection of mail from rail and sea, consulates hosting diplomats, hansom cabs vying for the attention of foot-weary travellers, Admiralty officers parading along the town. Horses, stray dogs, beggars and stall owners all added to the vision, the sounds and smells of the coastal community that was always endowed with the fresh sea air swirling in and around its houses, docks, and seashore. The rail service that operated in the town had done so since 1862 and every train brought a new consignment of soldiers, sailors, emigrants and travellers to the town.

Most of the buildings that stood directly on the seafront had maritime uses. Shipping companies like the German Lloyd Line, the White Star Line, the Inman Line and many more were strung out along the seafront with their jetties and piers protruding towards the natural deep-water channel that ran immediately in front the town and parallel to the town's main street. It is estimated that millions of emigrants threaded these streets and piers in the haemorrhage of Irish people that left the country over decades. In the dead centre of the town two large cambers offered refuge for small boats from the main harbour waterway where they could moor in relative safety.

The main population of the town lived in the outlying suburbia that stretched from behind the seafront façade, drifting around St Colman's Cathedral and reaching back to the townlands that then became farmlands, making up the rural landscape of Great Island. In the townland of Clonmel, less than a mile from the cathedral, the Old Church cemetery had been in use for centuries and contained the graves of many military, business, literary, ecclesiastical and civic figures that had featured in the life of the town.

Almost adjoining one of the cambers was the office of the Cunard shipping company. Cunard were the owners of RMS *Lusitania*. The company had been founded in 1840 and had set up a regional office in Cobh as early as 1867. Several different locations were used before they settled in the redbrick building that was positioned in the centre of town and close to the camber. There was a sturdy pier at the back of the building and a canopied area where passengers awaiting embarkation could stand under and keep out of the rain. In earlier days, when time did not seem to press so heavily upon the operations of trans-Atlantic travel, sailing ships moored right alongside the pier in close proximity to the building. However, as the need for speedy delivery of goods and people came to dominate movement between the continents, the practice emerged whereby passengers would be brought out by ferry from the shipping company pier to the entrance of the harbour so that they would be there and waiting for the passenger liner as it arrived. This saved time and money and it was often the case that passengers were out and ready to board their liner long before it appeared. Later observers were to wrongly conclude that the harbour wasn't deep enough to accommodate the larger steamships but it was really about timesaving. Many thousands of passengers would have embarked from the pier at the back of the Cunard office over the years. Few of them would have imagined that in May of 1915 the canopy at the back of the building would be filled with coffins containing the innocent victims of an attack on a Cunard ship.

The people of Cobh had been accustomed for many years to the coming and goings of shipping merchants, crews and passengers. Like any seaport the harbour area and its approaches had seen many incidents and sometimes tragedies involving groundings, storm wreckage, loss of life and accidental deaths but to this day the RMS *Lusitania* was the greatest consequential seafaring tragedy to impact on the town and its people.

2

Submarines and
Submarine Warfare

When the RMS *Lusitania* was struck by the torpedo and sank in only eighteen minutes, there were those that thought this was a new and deadly form of warfare. In fact, the idea of sub-maritime activity had been around for a long time. The notion of people exploring the depths of the ocean is not a new one. From ancient times men have dived beneath the waves in search of food. Sometimes it was for pearls or even for leisure. Whole cultures, particularly on Pacific Islands and in the Caribbean, sustained themselves from the sea. In the evolution of cultures and conflict perhaps it's not surprising that men would eventually take warfare and tactics beneath the waves. After all, surface fleets built and designed for battle had been a feature of organised cultures from the earliest of times. The Greeks deployed huge fleets of ships to defend their nation states and expand their influence. There are records of extensive sea battles complete with naval strategic manoeuvres adorning the accounts of this sophisticated culture. However, battleships at the time were simply used to deliver soldiers to a location and were seen solely as a delivery platform for fighting men.

It is not clear when undersea warfare was first considered. There are claims that Alexander the Great was lowered beneath the waves in a glass barrel in AD 337[1] and while many military strategists must have pondered the advantage of commanding the depths, it wasn't until later centuries, particularly the nineteenth and twentieth, that sub-surface craft were considered to be worth exploring and developing. The military advantages of an unseen weapon capable of striking from beneath the sea may seem very obvious today but it was some time before naval commanders were convinced that such vessels could be viable and effective.

Multiple challenges confronted those inventors who had to grapple with problems of watertight integrity, sufficiency of breathable air, withstanding of pressures in excess of atmospheric levels and the operation and fitting of propulsion and steering mechanisms. The addition of weaponry would further complicate the design and construction of such vessels. Early designs were little more than deep-hulled rowing boats with raised gunnels. The American War of Independence was the backdrop to the design of an egg-shaped wooden vessel that was crewed by one man who was able to power it by manually operated propellers and oars. The brainchild of David Bushnell (1740–1824), this little submarine was meant to threaten the British fleet imposing a blockade on New York in 1776. It was named the *Turtle*. Early features supposedly included the ability of the operator to admit water in controlled amounts to the bilge of the vessel to assist descent. Externally fitted ballast could be detached from inside the vessel to facilitate ascent in case of emergency.[2] Most importantly perhaps it was claimed that the vessel could carry and detach munitions that could be used to cause explosive damage to ships at anchor. There appears to be little success recorded in the use of this vessel as a weapon of war.

A fellow American built on Bushnell's interests and began addressing the building of submarines himself. Having lived in France in the late 1790s, Robert Fulton (1765–1815) was initially encouraged by the French Government to develop an underwater ship over 20ft in length which was to be called the *Nautilus*. In 1800 he met with Napoleon to copper-fasten French support for his vessel which he argued could be most effective in offensive operations against the British Fleet. *Nautilus* successfully descended to a depth of 24ft having been tested in the Seine River and later at sea off Cherbourg. During sea trials an explosive charge was towed behind the submarine to prove that it was capable of delivering a lethal load.

Despite the apparent success of Fulton's creation in remaining operational beneath the surface of the water, he did not receive unambiguous support from the French authorities. Later he tried to persuade British Naval authorities of the benefit of his invention for maritime defence and offence but the Admiralty remained unconvinced. Their opposition to the use of submarines for naval deployment remained the policy up until the nineteenth century. They were, however, impressed by his successful deployment of explosives during tests in England. When back in the United States, Fulton continued to work on refining his inventions until his death in 1815 and is credited with having merged the concept of the underwater vessel with an explosive device or torpedo.[3]

Coincidentally the first sub-sea vessel to reach the newly discovered location of the wreck of RMS *Titanic* just under 200 years later was also named the *Nautilus* and was led by a French exploratory team. Unlike its predecessor, the more recent vessel was capable of withstanding incredible pressures on the remote seabed some 4,000 metres below the surface of the North Atlantic. Numerous other European inventors created different styles and types of underwater vessels. Some tackled the issue of oxygen, others the pressure-resistant hulls. By the middle of the nineteenth-century a craft was built in the US that contained ballast tanks, an air compressor and a means to maintain oxygen levels while submerged. In many cases during these early pioneering periods inventors were lost, drowned or asphyxiated during trials. Improvements in steering mechanisms and propulsion continued over the nineteenth century often in different countries and under the direction of different inventors.

Navies had still not fully embraced the idea of using submarines in warfare. In addition to the whole reliability of the craft and the unknown problems they might face there was also the moral question of attacking a party from an unseen location. Some military officers felt this was immoral, although others argued that war was always unpleasant and advantages had to be taken whenever they presented themselves. A significant development in the use of a submarine as a weapon of war occurred during the American Civil War (1861–1865). A Confederate vessel, the *Hunley*, had been tried and tested with mixed results. During two of her four trials she sank with the loss of all crew.[4] She was later to successfully deliver a torpedo that sank the Union warship *Housatonic* off the coast of South Carolina. This is supposedly the first time that a submarine was successfully used to sink a ship during wartime.

One of the most influential designers of submarines was John Phillip Holland. He was born in County Clare in 1841. His designs were eventually adapted by both the US (who initially rejected them) and Great Britain. Holland was noted for being anti-British. After his plans had been rejected by the American Navy, the Fenian Brotherhood offered to fund the design of his submarine. The Fenians had been formed in the US with the intention of assisting in the ongoing struggle for Independence that Irish people sought. In Ireland the failure of the 1798 Rebellion against British Forces, the abolition by Britain of the Irish Parliament in 1801, the obscene loss of life during the Famine of 1845–1852 and the failure of another rebellion in 1848 were all contributing factors to the rise of the Irish Republican Brotherhood in the US. The idea was that Americans of Irish extraction would raise much-needed funds to arm those in Ireland willing to fight what they saw as the 'occupation' of a small distinct nation by its nearest, biggest neighbour, Great Britain. The 'Brotherhood' were happy to provide resources for the development of any product which could be used against Britain's Royal Navy and Holland's second submarine was named *Fenian Ram*.[5] After they lost interest another company funded the most recent design of the *Holland* in 1897 called the *Plunger* and it was successfully sold to the American Navy. This company was to eventually glean most of the benefits of Holland's design when it sold the prototype plans to the US in 1900 and later more to Great Britain. Holland is thought to have gained little from his inventions in terms of material wealth.

During these advances in the attitudes about the value of the submarine, the German Navy felt that these types of vessels were unproven. They had a proud naval heritage incorporating surface fleets and prior to the outbreak of the First World War, Admiral Aflred von Tripitz maintained that submarine experimentation was a waste of money.[6] The French, the British, the Russians and the Americans, who had all experimented with submarine development, had not deployed or equipped their navies with them; however, they began to change their approach in closing years of the nineteenth and the dawning of the twentieth century.

The US Navy started building a submarine fleet for full service in 1900, using the Holland prototype. The British introduced and deployed the A class submarine in 1904. Conditions were cramped and inhospitable for the crew members. They proved disastrous for the Royal Navy with three of the first five either sinking, disappearing, or causing fatalities. The A5 was brought to Cobh to showcase the vessel for the assembled Admiralty Southern Command. However, a flash fire caused the death of seven crew members, six of whom are buried in the Old Church Cemetery in Cobh. The German Navy, despite reservations, began to build submarines in 1906,[7] prompted by the construction by other nations such as France, Russia and others. By the outbreak of the First World War they had twenty-eight vessels; this was way below the number that had been produced by other navies but German technology was proving superior, with longer ranges at sea possible.

One of the most significant events to influence nations of the destructive value of the submarine came about on 22 September 1914. The German U9 successfully attacked and sunk three aging British Cruisers. The HMS *Aboukir*, HMS *Cressy* and HMS *Hogue* that had been patrolling together in the North Sea were spotted by Captain Otto Weddingen. In a period of just over forty-five minutes all three vessels were torpedoed and sunk with the loss of over 1,400 men. Only 837 survived the attack. The German submarine crew were hailed at home as heroes while British Admirals faced criticism in Britain. Initially, it had been claimed that the ships were sunk by mines. However, the true potential of the lethal capacity of the submarine had been very clearly demonstrated that day. This particular action may have played a part in the RMS *Lusitania* story. Seven months after it, the vulnerability of this type of old ship meant a Royal Navy cruiser was directed to flee away from the scene of the sinking RMS *Lusitania* and ordered to return back to Cobh. HMS *Juno* was an 'Eclipse' Class Light Cruiser that had been built and then launched in 1897. In August of 1914, already deemed to be an old ship, she was assigned as a constituent part of Cruiser Force E also known as the 11th Cruiser Squadron with four other similar vintage cruisers patrolling the southern entrance and approaches to the Irish Sea. The squadron, under the command of Rear Admiral Phipps Hornby, comprised of HMS *Juno*, HMS *Minerva*, HMS *Doris*, HMS *Venus*, and HMS *Isis*. Their area of operation, at least at the beginning of the war, extended out beyond the Fastnet lighthouse on the Atlantic shipping routes that approach Ireland. Their remit included the patrolling of this area to 'cover liners, cargo carriers and tramp steamers approaching the British Isles from the Atlantic'.[8] Despite the fact that these ships were on the front line of protecting merchant shipping, the information they received was very often at least twenty-four hours old. In the much-criticised handling of Admiralty intelligence, solid information on the activities and the movements of submarines in and near the western approaches was often not conveyed to the very ships charged with protecting merchant travellers from the dangers. It would appear that the Admiralty's fear of having the HMS *Juno* sunk by a submarine outweighed the humanitarian consideration of saving the lives of civilians. Rather than pick up passengers from the stricken ship and/ or engage with the enemy, a warship of the Royal Navy was to turn its back on both and flee to the safety of Cobh.

Every submarine class that was built in Germany and elsewhere benefited from improvements in design and capacity often brought about by bitter experience. The U20 submarine which was to attack RMS *Lusitania* was the second of the latest class built in a design that was intended to extend the reach of German U-boats into the furthest bounds of the oceans. Up to then many submarines had operated largely off coastlines. These were the first vessels to have diesel engines fitted.[9] These engines were more fuel efficient for long distances and were safer than their petrol counterparts. Conditions on these ships still remained uncomfortable and claustrophobic. Everything needed for survival of the crew, propulsion of the ship and the delivery of lethal weaponry had to be contained in the narrow confines of the cigar-shaped hull. Unlike surface vessels, where funnels, vents, masts, anchors, guns and boats could be stored outside, the submarine had no option but to have everything inside. Internally every centimetre of space was taken up with systems, machinery, pipework and the need to be able to store, house and load the 5m long torpedoes which were the main offensive weapon carried. Living quarters, facilities and space for the crew was a low priority in the overall design and sailors worked and lived in intimate proximity to their cramped mechanical environment. Fresh water, fresh air and fresh clothing became a distant memory as the extended sea patrols became longer.

It was not just German sailors who suffered dreadful claustrophobic confinement; almost all submariners battled with conditions that set them apart from conventional sailors and the relative comfort of surface ships. In addition to the adrenalin-filled terror of coming under fire during combat, submariners had to deal with the great fear of being entombed at the bottom of the ocean if their vessel was struck or disabled. A lingering death by asphyxiation was the constant fear among those who served under the sea.

Despite the uncertainty of the effectiveness of submarines by the outbreak of the First World War they were already present in many fleets. One estimate suggests Britain had seventy-three, the French had between sixty-seven and seventy-five, the Russians had twenty-two deployed in the Baltic and the Black Sea, the Italians about twenty, the United States eighteen, the Japanese had twelve, the Austrians had five and even the Greeks boasted a fleet of two submarines.[10] Later claims by some countries that submarine warfare was underhanded and unfair don't have credibility when one considers the widespread acceptance by navies of the world for the need to complement their surface fleets with submarines. Given the cost of building such vessels, there must have been a compelling belief of the necessity to include submarines in their arsenal of fighting vessels.

To this day submarines remain an integral part of naval fleets around the world. They have evolved far beyond the simplistic first attempts to stay submerged. The size and sophistication of today's vessels appear to know no bounds. There are submarines that can stay submerged for six months or more. There are those that can submerge and remain beneath the earth's frozen icecaps. Many of them carry lethal warheads that can be launched from one continent to another from any ocean. Some of them are driven by nuclear power and others carry weapons of mass destruction of a size and power that could only have been dreamed about by the navies of the First World War. Despite the early rejection of strategists for these vessels, despite the reluctance by some to have them engaged as weapons of war, the submarine, with all its lethal and secretive power, is here to stay. There are few oceans of the world today that are not patrolled and populated by these gigantic sophisticated underwater ships.

Shipping Companies and Trans-Atlantic Passage

By the arrival of the twentieth century, the competition among shipping companies offering trans-Atlantic passenger services had resulted in a raft of new ships with advanced designs, speeds and services. Europeans emigrated in their millions to North America and what they were willing to pay for their journeys became the income that drove companies to invest in vessels that could carry ever more people with a faster turn-around time between continental Europe and North America. In earlier times the speed of a ship was dependent on the ever-changing natural forces of wind and tide. Without the use of long-range forecasts and satellite navigation, captains often relied on hunches about the proximity of storms and conditions at sea. There was a more leisurely approach to travel. As the nineteenth century progressed, speed became all important. In addition to the general consciousness about getting things done as quickly as possible, there were increasing business pressures in the whole area of commercial communication.

The delivery of mail became subjected to consideration of timing. Shipping companies were now not just competing for passengers but also for being the fastest to convey mail across the Atlantic

Ocean to facilitate truly international and global business. Mail was the main form of communication. Business could not be conducted without it. Mail was the way in which families kept in touch across vast distances. Everything and everybody from large government departments and global commercial enterprises, to individuals and families, communicated by letter. Although telegraphy, when it came, revolutionised communication, the simple letter was still the main means of communication and record. Even when a telegraphic message was received it still had to be committed to paper and often sent on the last leg of its journey by post or package. For shipping companies the contract gleaned to carry mail could mean the difference between viability or not. Ships like the RMS *Lusitania*, the *Titanic* before her and many others carried the lettering RMS preceding their names. This was a most public declaration that the ship was warranted to carry Royal Mail by appointment of the Queen or King of England. When initially built the caption would be SS for steamship which was a descriptive term of the type of ship it was. But RMS declared one of the functions and duties of the ship.

British-based shipping companies didn't just seek contractual arrangements from the indigenous business interests; they also sought contracts from international companies based in continental Europe to deliver their mail and goods to Britain, America and elsewhere. British ships could collect mail from any European company and deliver it to North America by stopping off along the way in French or Belgian ports where trains and roads connected with ships bringing passengers and always mail. Equally, European companies who wanted to send packages or mail to British destinations could send them via the trans-Atlantic liners which would drop off that mail in Cobh. It would be brought by rail from the south coast harbour town to Dublin on the east coast where it would be taken onto to its final leg of the journey to the sorting offices in London. Such was the growth of this industry that it resulted in fierce competition.

The increasing speed and grace of ships became a feature of commercial competition in attracting customers and business and assisting them in deciding which shipping company to travel with or who to entrust their precious mail and cargo to. Quite apart from commercial competitive concerns, the status and positioning of merchant fleets became a source of national pride. One of the most noted manifestations of this maritime competitive streak was the seeking of the Blue Riband, the title and trophy that was awarded to the fastest passenger liner to cross the Atlantic. The points of reference were Bishop's Rock off the Scilly Isles near the English Channel and Ambrose Light in New York Harbour. Shipping companies pitted themselves against each other to win the right carry the prestigious prize and in doing so earn the right to fly the treasured blue pennant on their masts. The practice of awarding the Blue Riband went on from 1860 to the middle of the twentieth century.

Colin Clifford, who made the Blue Riband the subject of his academic studies, created a table of the winners and the years of award.[1] Clifford lists the ships who captured the prize and details the average speed that they made between the two points of reference. It was German shipping companies who dominated the Riband holders list from 1898 to 1907. The last British ship to hold the award prior to that year was the Cunard liner *Lucania*. She had been built in 1893 as a sister ship to *Campania*. She established a new record on her maiden voyage of an average crossing speed of 22 knots and continued on the Liverpool to New York route until she was irrevocably damaged by fire when berthed at her pier after which she was scrapped. This occurred after she had lost the Blue Riband to the *Kaiser Wilhem Der Grosse*, a ship of the North German Lloyd Line which improved the crossing speed to an average of 22.4 knots in 1898. The *Deutschland* of the Hamburg-Amerika Line sped across at an average speed of 24 knots to capture the prize in 1900. Later that year the *Kronprinz Wilhelm* of North German Loyd Line retook the Riband for their company by a tiny margin of .75 knots and the following year kept it in house when the *Kaiser Wilhelm II* barely exceeded it to hold the title at 24.8 knots. Then from 1901 to 1907 the German companies remained the dominant force in the prestigious competition with the *Kronprizessan Cecilie* maintaining the lead for German shipping with a continued average speed of 25 knots. That was until the RMS *Lusitania* came along. In 1907 the

RMS *Lusitania* established a new record making an average 25.57 knots completing the journey in under five days. Britain finally had recaptured the initiative and the Riband from their German rivals.

This competitive activity was symptomatic of a much broader and far more serious competition between Great Britain and Germany. Over the preceding centuries Britain had claimed they ruled the waves. This was no hollow claim. The Royal Navy had commanded the oceans for many years, defeating formidable naval fleets of Spain, France and others in the pursuit of expanding their respective empires around the world. Britain had prided herself on being a truly maritime nation, expanding her political influence to every corner of the globe. Other countries looked on in envy as the successes of the British fleet assisted the establishment of commercial hubs around the world and facilitated consolidation of colonies where they could extract natural resources not found at home. Everything from tea to spices and silver to gold were brought back to the home country to increase and develop its power and influence on the world stage.

Being an island nation, the provision of a powerful navy was also a necessity for the defence of the epicentre of the realm that was England. By the nineteenth century there had been a rule of thumb policy that the Royal Navy should be maintained at a size that would exceed any other navy afloat by being a minimum of 2.5 times greater than its nearest rival. As the reign of Kaiser Wilhelm got under way he vowed that he would not see Britain holding onto this powerful position on the oceans of the world and so ordered the dedicated construction of a naval and merchant fleet that would rival that of the Royal Navy in power, reach and effectiveness. Despite the fact that Wilhelm was directly related to British Royal family there was an apparently nasty rivalry between the families of both monarchs. It would develop into a national suspicion that ultimately contributed to the two countries unleashing lethal force against each other's subjects on the blood-soaked fields and cities of Europe. What compelled the German, British, Russian, and Austrian aristocracies to unleash the widest and most destructive conflict that the world had ever witnessed? Not only did they manage to end some of their own empires but they collectively cost the lives of somewhere in the region of 20 million of their subjects too.

The building of the RMS *Lusitania* came about against a background of fierce competition between the shipping companies, particularly between German and British merchant fleets on the trans-Atlantic passenger routes. Germany had held the Blue Riband for the last few years. It was a matter of pride that Britain should recapture it. Another consideration for Britain was the fact that an increasing number of shipping companies were being amalgamated and bought up by American commercial interests. J.P. Morgan, a US shipping magnate, with his International Mercantile Marine corporation would become the major shareholder of the White Star Line. From a British Government and military perspective, this meant that the merchant fleet would not necessarily be at the disposal of Britain in future conflicts. Relying on the civilian merchant fleet in time of war was an important feature of strategic Defence policy. It was in this context that the subsidisation of the Cunard Company's building of the RMS *Lusitania* and the *Mauretania* came about. Because they wanted to build the ships simultaneously, two separate dockyards were to be used. The RMS *Lusitania* would be built in the Brown shipyard on the Clyde river in Scotland and the *Mauritania* in a yard in England. Even though the RMS *Lusitania* was supposedly a civilian passenger liner, the type and shape of the hull was the subject of military input and considerations. In order to acquire the heavy government subsidy, the shipping company had to agree to modify construction so that the ship could be utilised in time of war as a 'merchant cruiser'. In other words, a ship that could be used in a military capacity in time of war. Jones, Walsh-Johnson and Peeke describe it thus: 'So it was that the RMS *Lusitania* was conceived, out of the Royal Navy's need and with the British public's money'.[2]

This was not a new idea in Europe. Germany had already done the same and a number of their passenger liners were earmarked as merchant cruisers too. Like RMS *Lusitania*, some would be sunk during the war. The effect of the Admiralty input into the design of the RMS *Lusitania* instituted widespread and significant changes to the type of ship built. In effect, the hull of the ship was built largely within the parameters of that which would be required for a full military naval cruiser. The number of watertight compartments dividing the length of the hull, the capacity to isolate different propulsion areas and the construction of a second inner hull were all design features more applicable to a military vessel that a civilian

RMS *Lusitania* in Cork Harbour. (Courtesy *Cork Examiner*)

passenger ship. Jones, Walsh-Johnson and Mitch Peeke also suggest that the main deck was designed in such a way as to be able to bear the weight of heavy artillery in case a decision was made to use and arm the ship during time of war under the command of the Admiralty. The one area where the military specifications benefited the civilian considerations of the ship was in its inherent speed. The hull of the RMS *Lusitania* was built in the same sleek, narrow fashion of naval vessels that contributed greatly to the overall speed of the ship. The slender hull sliced through the sea with less resistance than a wider hull would create. This design feature allowed the ship to reach speeds that placed her at the forefront of the passenger trans-Atlantic 'race' that preoccupied the shipping companies of the day. Not surprisingly, the propeller type and arrangement, the propulsion engines and the positioning of the rudders were all designed with the concept of speed and manoeuvrability that may be required in time of war. Such was the ship that rolled down the slipways in Scotland.

Launched on 7 June 1906 by Lady Inverclyde, the RMS *Lusitania* was a hybrid, a half civilian/half military creation that could recapture Britain's pride in peace time while becoming a serious military asset in time of war. Although it would be another eight years before the outbreak of war, the design and dual capacity of the ship would have been known to the German maritime industry and of course the German military machine. Given the £2.6 million subsidy donated by the British Government it was a feature of the ship's operational availability that the Admiralty would always have a call on the ship. And prior to the sinking of it there were other occasions during the war when the ship was called upon to carry munitions from the United States to Great Britain. Paddy O'Sullivan, researching this element of the ship's history, revealed in his book that an examination of the RMS *Lusitania*'s manifest on the previous voyage before it was attacked on 7 May 1915, showed the carriage of munitions in similar amounts to that on her last one. He explains:

> This was not the first time that the RMS *Lusitania* shipped munitions; an examination of her cargo manifest for her

penultimate voyage reveals a very similar shipment. White Star
liners and others also assisted in transporting munitions to feed
the insatiable demands of war. During the early stages of the war
Britain repeatedly under-estimated the enormous amount of
munitions required daily for her troops and was obliged to rely
on the United States armament manufacturer, Bethlehem Steel
Corporation, to fill the void.[3]

So, once again, one must consider the idea that while RMS *Lusitania*
may well have been in the business of carrying civilian passengers,
the ship also had a very important military role. The question arises
as to how well-informed passengers were that they were travelling
on what some could consider a semi-military ship and if not that, a
ship with a distinctively military mission. Instead of the passengers
being asked to pay for the privilege of a civilian voyage perhaps
they should have been paid to complete the decoy of a military
mission on a seemingly innocent ship. A present-day analogy might
be construed as follows. A US airline company offering flights into
Tehran for business and pleasure purposes after Al Qaida or some
such body had placed newspaper adverts in *The New York Times* that
they will target any US plane entering their airspace. The company
knowingly taking payment off passengers, loading the plane with
high explosives for delivery to the military and flying them to
Tehran while claiming their aircraft could outrun the speed of any
Tehran based aircraft which was waiting there for them! Would such
a scenario play out today?

   Whatever the specifications that were laid down by the Admiralty
in the construction of this ship, it is its use for delivery of lethal
munitions that brought its passengers into danger.

4

The First World War

It became fashionable in the years and decades after the sinking of the RMS *Lusitania* to portray it as an isolated incident that shattered peace and led America into the war, that the numbers killed were on a scale not ever seen before. The fact is that the mechanised slaughter of millions of people across Europe had been going on since the First World War began in August of 1914.

In simplistic narratives in Ireland and Great Britain at the time, the war was often seen as a British response to the aggressions of Germany. The reality of course is far more complex. The catalyst for the outbreak of the war was undoubtedly the assassination of the Austrian Archduke Ferdinand and his wife in Sarajevo on 28 June 1914. He was the heir to the throne of the Austria-Hungarian Empire. The killer was a Bosnian Serb named Gavrilo Princips[1] and the action was one that was set against a background of long-running ethnic and political conflict in the Balkans. The problem was that by 1914 the main powers and empires across Europe and Russia had taken positions of alliance and support that resulted in a very delicate and vulnerable balance of power in the world as it was known then. It seemed now that the line-up of powers were bristling with intent, shaping up against each other and spoiling for a fight. Previous wars of the nineteenth century and earlier had often been small regional affairs that didn't last too long. In fact, many people thought that what became known as the Great War would be over by Christmas. On one side the 'Central Powers' of Germany were allied to Austria-Hungary who were engaged in a bitter dispute with the Slavic state of Serbia. On the other side France, Russia and Great Britain formed the 'Triple Entente'.

Austria-Hungary categorised Serbian actions in their jurisdiction as terrorism and criticised the Serbian government for inaction and compliance. The Russian Empire, however, pledged support to the Serbs in the event that Austria-Hungary should move against them. Three weeks after the Archduke was murdered an ultimatum was issued to the Serbian government that made demands many felt would be impossible to comply with. The tone and content of the ultimatum was worded in such a way that it led a British diplomat to remark he 'had never before seen one State address to another independent State a document of so formidable a character'.[2] Although Serbia agreed to most of the document it did not satisfy Austria-Hungary and war was declared against Serbia on 28 July 1914. Russia immediately announced its intention to mobilise its massive army in defence of Serbia. On 1 August, Germany, which was formally allied to Austria-Hungary, declared war on Russia. France, allied to Russia, now found itself in a state of war against Austria-Hungary and Germany. Having a contingency in place for such an eventuality, Germany began to implement her 'Schlieffen Plan' which would see her army march through the small state of Belgium to take up positions in France. Great Britain, bound by an early nineteenth-century treaty with Belgium responded to a request by the Belgian King to come to their defence and so declared war on Germany on 4 August. This automatically put her at war with Austria-Hungary too. As the formality of alliances clicked into place one after the other, the consequential effect was that the entire continent of Europe would become the stage for the most destructive war ever to take place. Literally millions of soldiers began to mobilise for a conflict that would traumatise entire generations and herald the end of empires, kings and aristocracy. The value of human life and the integrity of the human body would be disintegrated in the carnage that was to follow. Within a few days of the German Army arrival in Dinant Belgium, 612 men, women and children were assembled and shot in the main town square to send a chilling message to those Belgian civilians who sought to resist German occupation.[3]

It was the confluence of events that took place in places like Sarajevo, Belgrade, Paris, Berlin, Brussels, Moscow and London that all led in one way or the other to the death of almost 1,200 people on RMS *Lusitania* on 7 May the following year. There were many on board that day who had no knowledge of the events that would lead to their demise. Ireland at the time was still a part of Great Britain and huge numbers of Irish men (including the author's grandfather) were to fight over the following four years in British Army uniforms on the battlefields of France and elsewhere. Despite this reality there was a growing demand in Ireland for Independence. Multiple subversive, political and diplomatic efforts in and from Ireland over the course of the previous century had failed to bring about the return of Ireland's own parliament which had been abolished by Britain in the Act of Union of 1801. Promises of Home Rule for Ireland had been made by Great Britain but failed to materialise and it must have seemed ironic to some that Britain's call to arms for soldiers in the First World War made reference to the defence of small nations from the larger neighbouring aggressors. Many in Ireland felt that Britain's presence in the country was exactly that. Some groups who were determined to get Britain to leave Ireland by force of arms, perceived the First World War as a possible opportunity in which they could strike a blow for Independence for themselves. It was in this regard that some activists for independence courted the favour of Germany and felt common cause in its war against Great Britain.

5

Blockades and Retaliation

A n important early strategy of Britain at the outset of the First World War was to impose a blockade around the North Sea and consequently the German ports. The idea was to restrict German naval access to the oceans and also prevent war-making materials (contraband) from reaching Germany from the outside. The growth of the German Navy had been a matter of concern for the British for a number of years and a full 'Naval Race' had taken place whereby Britain stuck to a formula that she must, as a matter of national security, have a ratio of ships in her navy that exceeded any other. As an island nation, Britain placed inordinate importance on maintaining control of the high seas. At the start the twentieth century, German naval expansion and the increasing number of ships being built by them was the biggest threat to Britain's hugely dominant position of naval power. The Royal Navy fleet was an effective weapon of war that was capable of protecting British commercial and military interests around the globe. The British Empire stretched into all oceans and continents and the Royal Navy, for centuries, had been an integral part of the discovery and acquisition of colonies. It followed that they then became a crucial element in the subsequent maintaining and protection of them. The industrious lifeblood of Britain in her international export and import trade, the political influence of the country around the world, and the diplomatic influence that she exercised at virtually all levels of international relations were greatly aided by the ever-present services rendered by the Royal Navy. It was absolutely essential, therefore, that a rival country's fleet such as that which Germany's presented, would not surpass or extend its influence in a challenge to Britain's interests. This was an issue of primary importance to Great Britain. It was perceived in Britain that the German Navy represented a very real and present danger to Britain in the early years of the twentieth century leading up to the First World War.

Throughout history, as far back as the ancient Greeks, a regular strategy of warring nations was to neutralise the effectiveness of enemy fleets by blocking off access or exits of harbours where naval ships were based. In addition to neutralising an enemy's warships and conducting physical military attacks, it was also deemed legitimate to attack the commercial lifeblood of a foe. When this was put into effect it was known as a blockade. There were even general aspirational practices that accompanied the process of blockading. Where natural harbours featured narrow entrances of limited depth of water a blockade was easily put into effect. Enemy vessels stationed outside could easily pick off and sink any vessel trying to enter or leave. The sunken ship could then even aid the blockading force as it would become a navigational hazard, allowing nothing but the smallest of boats in or out.

In 1914 a close-proximity blockade of German ports was not an option for Britain; long-range, land-based weapons that could fire almost over the horizon, the use of coastal submarines and small, fast torpedo boats made this impossible. Thus it was decided that controlling the North Sea was the best option for Britain to inhibit the operational effectiveness of their enemy's fleet. Because their warships were not sitting immediately outside of German ports Britain could claim that what they were doing was not technically a blockade. Their surface fleets patrolled key access areas to the North Sea. Instead of completely blocking the entrance and exit into the North Sea, Britain declared the area a 'warzone' and claimed the right to stop and search neutral ships that intended to enter port as a national security issue. Under a generally accepted protocol in time of war known as the cruiser or prize rules, a belligerent vessel could stop and search a ship in a warzone to check it for 'contraband'. Contraband was any material such as munitions or explosives that could be used by the enemy in pursuit of its military objectives. The definition could be varied or expanded to include even steel or manufacturing material. In the case of the First World War, the longer the blockade continued the more Britain's interpretation of what constituted contraband was widened. It was to eventually include foodstuffs and materials used in the manufacture of food.[1]

The imposition of the British blockade involved heavy patrolling by Royal Navy ships between Norway and the Shetland Islands, between Dover and Calais, from the Orkneys to the Shetlands and a concentrated, regular patrolling of the eastern British seaboard up to 100 miles offshore. This was designed to control and contain access to the North Sea and protect the coastline of Great Britain. The impact of this was described by some as resulting in the entire area becoming the 'North Sea German prison'.[2] When materials used in the manufacture of food were not reaching their ports some in Germany called it the 'hunger' or the 'starvation' blockade. In addition to the presence of the Royal Navy ships on patrol, minefields were laid. The mines did not distinguish between allies or enemies and ships from both sides were sunk. In this way Britain maintained a stranglehold on all shipping into and out of German ports. The blockade inhibited and deterred not just military movement of German naval vessels, but also civilian ships who were trading with Germany.

Under the operation of blockades and in time of war there were general guidelines that countries were expected to observe. Warring nations were understandably entitled to attack naval vessels without warning and they were entitled to impede cargoes of weapons on civilian ships destined for their opponents. Hospital ships were supposed to be spared from attack and ships of non-participating countries in a conflict could not be impeded on the high seas unless they were on their way to an enemy port. If a nation was neutral in a conflict they were entitled to conduct free trade on any ocean. Britain's blockade of the North Sea forced neutral ships of Norway and elsewhere to subject themselves to scrutiny so that they might get an escort through the minefields laid by the Royal Navy. These actions were construed to be illegal and could be described as acts of piracy.

There was an expectation that if the civilian vessels of one country were to be stopped by another, certain procedures would be followed. The Declaration of London, discussed below, sought to consolidate and define these practices. By and large it was felt that if a naval ship found contraband on a civilian ship the military vessel maintained the right to seize or destroy the offending material, whether it was munitions of something used in the manufacture of weapons. They also extended the right of seizure or destruction of the ship itself. This was to ensure that a particular vessel would not be used repeatedly to carry war-making materials. If such an operational decision was made by the military commander at the scene there were particular procedures that were supposed to be followed to ensure the safety of the civilian crew and or passengers. It became the responsibility of the naval vessel to ensure the safe passage of all passengers to the nearest neutral port. This could be done by escorting the captured ship or by taking the non-combatants onto the arresting vessel and bringing them to safety. These types of policies always assumed that the civilians were not a threat to the naval vessels. Britain, by and large, followed these procedures when boarding civilian vessels attempting to enter the North Sea.

As the blockade deepened it became apparent that legitimate trade was being affected and other nations became aggrieved that while they had no part in the war, Britain was preventing them from conducting legitimate international trade. Chatterton later wrote: 'Britain, by her blockade; though she was careful not to call it that by name, had become unpopular internationally, and the position regarding Anglo-trade connection was fraught with peril.'[3] With the blockades in operation in the English Channel, some ships, that would ordinarily operate out of Southampton began, instead, to use Liverpool.

In addition to the intentional offensive blockade being imposed on access to German ports, Britain also felt the need to put protective measures in place to prevent attack by submarines on British shipping. As the Royal Navy was stretched in the pursuit of their massive blockade civilian trawlers and yachts were brought into action in the war at sea. They were used to tow driftnets to impede or snare submarines that might threaten the east coast ports such as Liverpool or Bristol. Some of the nets had mines attached and many of the yachts and trawlers were mounted with weapons. This was effectively bringing civilians onto the front line of the war. The questions arises then of the utilisation of apparently innocent vessels to actively engage with the enemy. From a British perspective this was a natural feature of any conflict. Everybody in it together: every person, civilian or military, making a contribution for the protection of their homes and their country. The result was that by the end of August 1914 twenty-one armed merchant cruisers had been commissioned and about 200 trawlers. Within four or five months of the outbreak of the war Britain had augmented her Royal Naval fleet with over 800 minor vessels which was to rise to over 3,500 by the end of the war.[4] From a German perspective the war at sea now involved the use of clearly civilian vessels to carry out defensive/offensive operations against them. Their capacity to impose blockades on British ports was being confounded by the use of civilian sea captains and fishermen manning vessels that could fire on such U-boats. A suspicion of all craft was then to be expected.

In the case of the RMS *Lusitania*, there was further room for suspicious intent from the time that she was built and the large subsidy made by the British government to build ships that could be used during any conflict as merchant cruisers. The problem with merchant cruisers was that while they were innocent vessels in peace time, carrying out their primary role of passengers or cargo ships, in time of war they became weapons of war, capable of inflicting lethal force on belligerent enemy vessels. Thus the idea of an innocent ship was influenced by the role she was playing in peacetime but it was equally influenced by the role she could possibly play during time of war.

The comprehensive blockading of the North Sea effectively choked off the German Navy's capacity to get out into the oceans of the world. In doing so it also prevented a reciprocal blockading by Germany of British ports, meaning the importation of weapons and war-making materials into Great Britain could proceed unopposed. Without the ability of mounting a similar blockade, Germany's options were limited. Retaliation came in the form of a different kind of blockade around the British Isles. Unlike the British use of mainly surface vessels, the Germans utilised their U-boats to impose the restrictions on merchant trade gaining access to Britain. The effectiveness of the submarine as a weapon of war against naval vessels had already been well established the previous September. Now it was to be used against civilian ships. On 4 February 1915 all waters around Britain and Ireland were declared by Germany to be a warzone. German submarines had already begun to target merchant vessels and up to that point had sunk ten British merchant ships.[5] Civilian ships of Germany's enemies and vessels of neutral countries were now officially warned of the dangers of entering the exclusion zones that were imposed.

Exclusion Zones, Q Ships and Warnings

O ne of the most innovative offensive strategies of the war against the German submarine was the 'Mystery' ships of the Royal Navy, also referred to as the 'Q' ships. Some claim that the Q stood for Queenstown but there could be other explanations there too such as simple lettering sequences in the absence of a fully-fledged State vessel under the white ensign.[1] Rear Admiral Gordon Campbell VC, wrote a book ten years after the war about his experiences in commanding Mystery ships. He attributes the idea to Vice-Admiral Sir H.W. Richmond, who he said was the first British Naval Officer to propose the use of such vessels in the First World War.[2] Julian Thompson suggests that the notion came to light from a cash-prize competition that was held in the Royal Navy which sought suggestions from personnel on how best to tackle the 'submarine menace'. Over sixty ideas were submitted, including vessels towing plane-shaped kites to deter U-boats, torpedo-fitted rowing boats and espionage agents planting bombs on the submarines.[3] Some of these were tried with varying degrees of success. One such idea was to disguise merchant ships as neutrals. Measures were taken by the Admiralty to arm merchant ships with guns or cannons which effectively brought civilians onto the frontline of the conflict. However, this tactic confused the operation of the system that had been applied in relation to how merchant ships would be treated during war time. With merchant ships now being armed, civilians were in danger not only of being sunk without warning but also being considered military targets if they engaged with the submarine. Other measures also placed civilians into danger. The Admiralty had advised British merchant shipping that plied waters where German submarines were thought to be operating to avoid major entrance to busy harbours, follow a zigzag course and in the event of sighting a submarine to ram it with all due haste.

Despite the inherent disadvantages of bringing civilians so directly into the path of danger, the statistics appear to show increased 'survivability' of those that were armed over those that were not. Throughout 1916 of the 310 British armed merchant ships that were attacked, 236 of them escaped and avoided destruction. This compared with only 67 out of 302 unarmed vessels that managed to escape.[4] Following the sinking of the RMS *Lusitania*, questions were raised as to why she had not been provided with an escort or been made part of a protective convoy system. The reality in 1915 was that the idea of convoy protection for civilian ships had not taken hold. It was felt by some in the Royal Navy that a convoy, with large number of ships travelling together, would present a bigger and therefore easier target for the submarine. By comparison, a single merchant ship with good speed and the deterrence of a mounted gun could stave off an attack by firing and forcing the U-boat to dive. Nevertheless the Admiralty did deploy a force of Royal Navy ships to patrol the approaches to the Irish Sea where merchant ship and passengers liners, having crossed the Atlantic, had to navigate in order to get to their destination. Given that submarines at the time had to be within a few hundred yards, and in a particular position to line up a torpedo shot for a ship, it is perhaps understandable that it was felt in some quarters that the speed of a ship alone was enough to deter an attack. The first deliberate convoy of merchant ships in May of 1917 only occurred after a change in leadership in the Admiralty.

The policy of arming civilian vessels was not confined to large merchant ships and the evolution of the tactic of Q ships was probably a natural progression from arming the larger merchants. In the case of a Q ship a nondescript vessel such as a coastal tramp or fishing boat would be fitted with heavy armaments with which to attack submarines. Deck-mounted weapons such as 3-inch artillery guns were positioned on the fore and aft decks of ships that otherwise looked like civilian, non-threatening vessels. Hoardings and boxes were constructed around the weapons and were made to appear like deck houses or machinery covers. They could be collapsed within seconds often by the operation of a single lever. They were crewed by experienced Royal Navy personnel who sought out submarines in areas where they were known to be operating. They then placed themselves deliberately in harm's way in order to get close to the U-boats. When submarine crews spotted these vessels they would adopt a leisurely approach to inspecting them as, on first appearances, they posed no threat. However, as soon as the submarine was within firing range, the gun coverings would be discarded and a rapid and sustained attack on the submarine would take place. The Germans were to refer to these vessels as 'trap ships'.

The modifications that were required to arm these vessels required military expertise as well as civilian know-how and a number of them were modified and converted in the naval dockyards of Cork Harbour. Some of them had huge quantities of hardwood loaded below decks into holds that would have previously been used for general cargo. It was thought such measures would assist the vessel in staying afloat if their enemy did get a chance to fire back. Other holds were often filled with coal so that they could stay longer at sea and operate further off shore if needed.

Their most important weapon was the element of surprise. It was known for these ships to adopt a series of strategies to get within effective range of the submarines. In the most banal situation these ships would steam offshore as if they were on an intended voyage, taking cargo from one port to another. Schedules of shipping companies that used regular routes were monitored and copied. Others operated as if they were fishing vessels, going to or coming from the abundant fishing grounds around Ireland. Another use of these secret ships was to have no armaments at all but to have what looked like trawling wire trailing astern as if they were fishing. In these cases a British submerged submarine was being towed. When a German U-Boat came to investigate the seemingly innocent surface craft, the British submarine could then attack the unsuspecting enemy without having had its presence revealed until the last possible moment. This ploy had its first successes in July 1915 when the fishing trawler *Taranaki* towed the British submarine C24 which successfully attacked and sank the German submarine U40. Later that month another trawler towing a different British submarine, the C27, torpedoed the German U23. Further success, involving both vessels towing submarines and those with just deck-mounted guns, was recorded in the following weeks. In a number of cases off the south coast of Ireland, Q ships were deployed as if they were civilian ships coming to the aid of vessels that had already been attacked by submarines, supposedly to recover crew from sinking vessels. Then when they were close enough and seemingly engaged in a humanitarian operation they could retaliate with fire of their own onto the surprised German submarine.

However innovative these methods were in successfully counteracting the threat of the submarines, one major disadvantage was that Germany could now insist that they were unable to distinguish between enemy vessels and civilian ships. Military targets such as naval destroyers, cruisers and frigates could easily be identified by their general shape, size and the flying of the naval ensign. In the case of Q ships, any type or shape of vessel, however big or small, with any flag at all could be carrying hidden weapons and deemed to be a possible threat.

Many of the Q ships operated out of Cork Harbour. They were crewed by a combination of Royal Naval personnel, civilian volunteers and Naval Reserve. They operated slightly outside of the naval command structure and were sometimes referred to in derogatory terms. One disadvantage in modifying these ships in Ireland rather than Britain was the fact that local Irish republicans who worked in the dockyards, and saw themselves involved in a struggle for independence from Britain, were aware of the deployment of these ships and could provide intelligence to German sources. Admiral Bayly referred to Cobh as: 'containing many spies doing what they could to damage England's endeavours, and where every ship and movement was closely watched'.[5]

In the pursuit of independence some perceived Britain's enemies as allies and there were numerous incidents in which Irish freedom fighters sought assistance from the German military machine. As a result of these fears, the ships and their crews had to maintain a deception to everybody, including most other members of the Royal Navy. When such vessels entered command areas like Cork Harbour they had to go through the whole routine of getting civilian customs clearance. When undergoing checks by the naval patrols that operated at the entrance, the senior officer would be advised and had to maintain strict secrecy. Sometimes the Admiral in Cobh was the only other person aware of the real identity and mission of these ships.

On board the Q ships there was always a designated routine, very much like what prevailed on Royal Naval ships. Captain's rounds took place whereby the captain or his executive officer carried out a thorough inspection of the ship every day and always by the captain himself on Sundays. This was to ensure operational efficiency of all equipment on board and cleanliness of every quarter, store and space which is the epitome of every navy ship. However, above decks ships were often left to look a little untidy to continue the ruse of it being a 'civvy' vessel. Despite their crews of trained men every attempt was made to make them look like innocent non-combatant vessels. Rear Admiral Gordon Campbell, who commanded one such ship, provided a detailed insight into the efforts that were made to keep up their disguise. He took command of a civilian coal ship and in the course of equipping for its role as a Q ship he had parts of the decks reinforced and modified to carry three 12-pounder guns. Such guns weighed about 12 cwt each. The guns were on deck but concealed by the gunnel that was also modified to have a section hinged which could be dropped down when the gun was brought into action. Depth chargers were also carried on board and, unlike many coastal trampers of the day, there was a wireless set fitted for communication with the Royal Navy/Admiralty. Side arms and rifles were also carried. Campbell also addresses the use of neutral flags. 'Another fairly simple guise was to fly neutral colours, a very old and perfectly legitimate *ruse de guerre*, provided the national colours were hoisted before opening fire'.[6] He explains that if a ship was to be deployed in a certain area and was seen repeatedly by a submarine suspicion would be aroused. To deter this a whole range of neutral flags were carried and plenty of coloured paint. The flags could be changed easily but they also painted different shipping company logos on the funnels of the vessels sometimes on a nightly basis. It became commonplace too for ships to construct large boards that were mounted on the hull of the ship painted as a flags and again many different neutral boards were held on-board. There was also attempts made to fool any submarine observers by adding certain shapes like funnels or masts. They were often put together with box wood and chicken wire but proved effective. These too could be erected or dismantled with ease to change the outline shape of the ship. In the case of the *Zylpha*, openings were cut out of bulkheads from one compartment to the next along the whole length of the ship.[7] These arrangements allowed the crew to move from any part of the vessel to another without being observed on deck, They could in this way get to and from the gun and other action stations without being seen. There were suggestions at one point that some of the men dress from the waist up like women to give the impression to inquisitive submariners that there were only civilians on board. It is not certain that this was ever done, but the men did get a clothing allowance to enable them purchase civilian clothing. When all preparations had been made the ship was renamed. Campbell and his refitted Q ship were assigned to Cobh, but operated out of Berehaven on the south-west Coast of Ireland.

The crews of Q ships had to undertake training for the type of warfare conducted by these secretive vessels. One confirmed tactic that was often used on these vessels was the orchestrated panic scene played out on board by crew members. The idea was that when a submarine appeared crew would run back and forth supposedly emulating the actions of fearful civilians and leading observers on the submarine to believe they had come across a boat with nothing but a group of frightened civilians on board. In the choreographed staging of these scenes, however, well-planned drills of preparing their guns for engagement were being undertaken. Part of the crew would board one of the ships boats, taking their belongings with them and the ship would appear to the enemy to be deserted. But, unseen on board, guns were made ready, munitions were placed in close proximity to them and gunners were getting to their station. The precious minutes gained by these choreographed drills were often the difference between successfully attacking the submarine and becoming a victim.

The *Farnborough*, the *Zylpha* and the *Baralong* (which had engaged and sunk two submarines) were all mystery ships that were stationed in Cobh. Chatterton provides a detailed narrative of one offensive action successfully concluded by Campbell and his converted coal ship:

> … Lt Commander Gordon Campbell in the Q ship Farnborough was steaming off the SW coast into the Atlantic when U68 was sighted awash about five miles away. Twenty minutes later came a torpedo which missed. Next the enemy broke surface and began shelling, so the Farnborough stopped, blew off steam and "abandoned ship", whilst Commander Campbell and his gun crews remained on board. The enemy closed to 800 yards and again fired, whereupon the Q ship dropped all disguise, replied with all three twelve pounders, hit the German several times and saw the U68 disappear. The Farnborough then steamed at her full speed of about nine knots over the position, dropped an explosive depth charge which caused the submarine to rise almost perpendicularly, displaying a large gash in her bows. At point blank range five more rounds were now fired into the conning tower so that once again the U-Boat disappeared. In order to make doubly sure two more depth charges were loosed off after which rose over the sea much oil and bits of wood.[8]

There were no survivors of the thirty-eight-man crew of the submarine and Campbell was promoted and decorated following the engagement. The case outlined demonstrates the full integration of civilian ships into the military strategy of Great Britain. The coal ship *Farnborough* dispatched the submarine and its crew with the effectiveness and determination of any warship.

It is important to note that while the success of the Q ship as an offensive weapon of war may not have been recorded before May 1915, they were in place and operational long before the sinking of the RMS *Lusitania* and were tasked with trying to achieve what the *Farnborough* had done when the opportunity arose.

Another operation of a Q ship deserves mention for its effectiveness and perhaps ruthlessness a little later in the war. On 19 August 1915 the Q ship *Baralong* was steaming off the Scilly Isles. A British steamer *Nicosian* had been stopped by the German submarine U27. The steamer's crew had taken to their boats and the submarine was preparing to shell the now empty ship.

> … The *Baralong* was flying the American flag. Approaching so that the *Nicosian* lay between herself and the submarine and so that the latter could not see what she was doing, the *Baralong* ran up the white ensign, unmasked her guns and trained them on the spot where the U27 would appear from behind the *Nicosian*'s bows. As soon as she did appear she was shelled at 600 yards and sunk at once.[9]

The *Baralong*'s commander reported that a search of the *Nicosian* found six of the submarine crew who all died as a result of injuries sustained during the initial shelling of U27. American crew members of the *Nicosian*, however, gave a rather different version in affidavits to the State Department of the US:

> Twelve of the submarine's crew escaped and made for the *Nicosian*. Some were shot and killed in the water and others as they clambered up the *Nicosian*'s side. Then the *Baralong* sent a

party of marines to hunt down the remainder with orders to take
no prisoners …[10]

In Chatterton's account of this incident he doesn't mention anybody
getting off the submarine and simply states that there were no
survivors.

> … before the German could make off, thirty four shells were fired
> from the Baralong and most of them scored hits. Within less than
> two minutes U27 and Wegener disappeared, never again to be
> seen by human eye. There were no survivors.[11]

Merchant vessels of all shapes and sizes were an integral part of the
war effort against submarines. Even those that were not armed were
prevailed upon to send the Admiralty positions of submarines that
were sighted. Whatever about the tactical wisdom of deploying these
vessels, there would be no mercy shown by submarines if the shape
of a gun was spotted or if their ruse of panic was detected. They were
sitting ducks. Despite their vulnerability, the Q ships did record some
successes and sank a number of submarines. But their effectiveness
inevitably diminished as time went on. For those submarine
commanders who did survive an encounter with them, the word
soon went round that what might look like an ordinary boat could
well be one that carried weapons that could damage a submarine
and endanger its crew or sink it entirely. So even if a ship was not
a designated merchant cruiser, even if a ship was not one that was
carrying munitions or explosives to an enemy, even if a ship carried
a neutral flag, there was no guarantee that it would not be capable of
attacking a German submarine. The point came when every vessel
encountered was a cause for suspicion. And while the British may
well have viewed this as the widespread protective deployment of
vessels for the protection and safety of their coastline and ships, the
German saw it as subterfuge which increased the threat to the safety
of their submarines and their crews.

Access to and from the North Sea was inhibited by the effective
British blockade and, with the German surface fleet thus confined,

they were left with no choice but to use sub-surface vessels in order to try and reduce the flow of imported arms, munitions and materials into Great Britain from abroad that were designated for use against Germany. The use of civilian ships as weapons of war by the British against German submarines prevented the usual cruiser rules being operated where the U-boat would have to approach and inspect the boat. Even if they were free to approach a civilian vessel that was not a 'trap ship' or Q ship and they discovered arms or munitions, they did not have enough space on a submarine to take passengers off the target ship and bring them to safety. Their setting up of the exclusion zone around Ireland and Britain and their warning of February 1915 to all merchant ships entering the zone, would have been seen by them to have given fair warning. Merchant ships of Great Britain and other nations at war with Germany would have been made aware of the threat. The decision firstly to enter the zone and secondly to carry munitions on board when doing so was known to have been a risk. This was a risk being taken by the Cunard shipping company and the British Government through her Ministry for Defence and Admiralty. If there was a risk implied in the decision to send the ship into the warzones with arms or munitions, surely there is an equal responsibility that must be accepted based on the decision in the first place if something goes wrong?

Less direct but also relevant, was the existing practice of using civilian vessels not just to carry war making-materials but also to use some of them as offensive ships capable of attacking and destroying an enemy vessel. The fact that this threat was there inevitably influenced the actions of submarines in encountering civilian ships and again this strategy implies a certain responsibility for those who adopted and implemented it. None of the inquiries that took place appear to have considered the negative impact of utilising civilian vessels in this way and how their use may impact on responsorial strategies of belligerents. It is difficult to know whether or not the existence of the Q ships heightened the relentless submarine campaign against civilian vessels in the declared warzone but their disguises, ruses and secrecy certainly influenced the way in which a submarine could engage with them when they encountered each other.

Cobh was a major port of operation for the Q ships under the Queenstown Command but they were also deployed around mainland Great Britain and Scotland too. The great harbour at Cobh provided a natural protection from the Atlantic Ocean but also from the threat of marauding enemy ships. The narrow entrance meant that the harbour and the ships that berthed and anchored there were well protected.

7

Cargo and Contraband

A general perception still exists that there are some questions about whether RMS *Lusitania* was carrying arms or not. The RMS *Lusitania* was carrying a large consignment of munitions and war making material. That is a fact. Passenger liners did not just carry passengers. While they may have been primarily advertised for this function, the carriage of cargo and mail were a critical part of their capacity to earn income. Glossy advertising posters of the day depicted graceful liners that were like floating palaces. Images of first-class dining rooms and beautifully appointed suites were emphasised in the attempts to attract influential passengers. However, these ships also had large dreary holds where commonplace cargo could be carried. Ships, by law, had to declare the cargo they carried and there were customs officials whose job it was to ensure that everything that went on board a ship in a port was documented and declared. Ships owners had to submit manifests which listed all items of cargo. There were certain items that were prohibited on certain ships. This was to do with trade, taxes, duties and safety of passengers. Manifests were submitted to customs officials in advance of the sailing time and date of a ship. The preliminary manifest would often include those items that were known to have been ordered or booked onto the ship long before departure date. Also included would be supplies for the ship itself. Supplementary manifests were designed, as the name suggests, to supplement the main manifest and were usually processed just before sailing. This allowed commercial interests to keep their intentions quiet until the last moment. This also applied to items being taken on board that an enemy might deem to be contraband.

The manifest of RMS *Lusitania* for her departure on 1 May 1915 from New York was fairly typical of the time. The items listed would be stowed in the cavernous holds reserved for cargo. Under the provisions of the agreement between the Cunard shipping company and the British Government and Admiralty there were certain holds that would be given over for exclusive use by the Admiralty in time of war should it become necessary. The primary boarding manifest listed a diversity of items such as brass sheets, copper wire, cheese, beef, lard, typewriters, butter, oysters and more. But, in the middle of the list, is '1,271 boxes of ammunition'. These were .303 Remington rounds that were the standard issue to soldiers of the British Army who were fighting in France. Peeke, Jones and Walsh-Johnson maintain the RMS *Lusitania* had more munitions than normal on the day.

> On her final voyage, she was carrying considerably more contraband than usual, including eighteen cases of fuses for various calibre artillery shells, which were listed on her manifest, and a large consignment of gun-cotton, an explosive used in the manufacture of propellant charges for big-gun shells, which wasn't listed on the manifest.[1]

They note that when these items became known about in America, they caused a minor sensation in the press. The authors explain:

> The gun-cotton was quite a large consignment and was stored in part of the new space created by the Admiralty, forward on E deck. It is worth recording that this large consignment was not packed in the proper containers usually employed to transport this explosive, due to a sudden shortage of them. According to the

original ship's manifest, the 1, 271 cases of ammunition that are listed on page one of the manifest right, are actually '1,248 cases of shrapnel' (supposedly just the lead musket balls with which to fill shrapnel shells). Also, the large consignments of Lard, Butter and Cheese mentioned on page one of this manifest were actually consigned to the Royal Navy's Weapons Testing Establishment at Shoeburyness, Essex and they were not stored in the refrigeration hold purely because the consignments were far too large to go into that hold! Quite why such an establishment would want some ninety tons of therefore rancid dairy products has never been explained.

The authors add further light to the bare description on the ships manifest for the munitions:

The 1,248 cases of shrapnel came from the Bethlehem Steel Corporation, and their shipping note was a little more specific than the ship's cargo manifest. The shipping note, dated 28 April 1915, shows 'consignment number 23' as being '1,248 cases of three-inch calibre shrapnel shells, filled; four shells to each case'. These shells were consigned to the Royal Arsenal at Woolwich and as our own subsequent research, aided by the Royal Artillery Historical Trust has revealed, they were for use by the Royal Artillery in the 13-pounder field gun. So why was such a large consignment of live artillery shells being carried aboard the RMS *Lusitania*, a passenger liner?[2]

If Britain felt justified in preventing not just arms and munitions getting into Germany but foodstuffs and manufacturing goods too, had not Germany the right to intercept the carriage of the deadly cargo described above? Some argued that Britain's methodology was targeting the goods rather than the passengers on board ships that were stopped by the Royal Navy and that property was replaceable but people were not. These were valid perspectives; however, as has been pointed out, the non-availability of the German Navy outside of the North Sea meant that only submarines could be used to effectively stop arms getting to Britain. If the submarines did not have the space to take passengers from munitions-carrying merchant ships all they were left with was the option to provide ample warning.

8

Attack in the Afternoon

The 7 May 1915 was a pleasant sunny day off the south coast of Ireland and it must have seemed to many passengers to have been almost holiday-like. RMS *Lusitania* had taken more than six days to cross the Atlantic, though it could easily have done it in less; wartime coal rationing meant that speed had been sacrificed for fuel saving. In addition, the ship had encountered fog as it approached the south coast of Ireland, causing it to reduce its speed even more, from a cruising speed of 18 knots to about 15. When the fog lifted the ship was in sight of the coast of Cork and less than 15 miles offshore. Farmers tilling their land and tending to their cattle would have seen great ships like the RMS *Lusitania* passing back and forth along the shipping lanes from their fields on a regular basis. The outlying headland of the Old Head of Kinsale contained a lighthouse which had served mariners for many years and become a major navigation point for shipping. If the wind was in the right direction on such days it was often possible to smell the lush grass and vegetation a few miles offshore. On sunny days, passengers on trans-Atlantic crossings often took the opportunity to go for a stroll on board. By 2 p.m. lunch was always finished and passengers had the opportunity to explore and stroll or to sit in and listen to some ship's entertainment.

While such activities were taking place on RMS *Lusitania* a very different scenario was being played out just a few hundred yards away that afternoon. Unseen by any passengers on board, the German submarine U20, under the command of Kapitanleutnant Walther Schwieger, lurked beneath the waves. Schwieger had been born into German nobility in April of 1885. In 1903 he joined the equivalent of the Navy Cadets and pursued a career in the German Navy. Having completed his training, he served on a number of torpedo boats and was promoted to Oberleutnant in 1908. He was posted to a light cruiser and later in 1911 was posted to the submarine section. Schwieger served on the U14 and after promotion took command of the U20 in the closing months of 1914.[1] On the afternoon of 7 May he was now six months in command of U20. RMS *Lusitania* was now 11 nautical miles off the Old Head. Unlike the leisurely activity on the passenger ship, the submarine was a hive of activity, preparing for military engagement. Sailors not on watch had been rousted from their bunks and, as on all naval vessels, everybody had a place to be and a particular task to perform during action stations. This same scene had played out frequently on the submarine in the preceding few days. U20 had patrolled down the west coast of Scotland and Ireland to take up station off Bristol in the Irish Sea. A couple of days prior to the arrival of the RMS *Lusitania* they were off the south coast in close proximity to Cork Harbour and the coastal port of Kinsale. On 5 May the U-boat spotted and sunk a small sailing vessel called the *Earl of Lathom*. Crew were ordered off the ship and it was sunk using explosive charges. Given the cost and expense of the huge torpedoes, captains were instructed to use less costly devices such as their deck-mounted guns or explosives where possible to disable and sink ships of a smaller type. Later that day U20 attempted to sink a vessel off Cork Harbour called *Cayo Romano*, but without success. The ship escaped the attentions of the submarine and made it safely to Cobh where the Admiralty was informed, after which they sent a general message to all at sea that there was a submarine operative in the area.

On 6 May two other vessels were attacked by the U20. The 4,000-ton *Candidate* and the similarly sized *Centurion* were sunk by torpedo just one day before the RMS *Lusitania* was due to arrive in the area. Questions inevitably arose later about whether RMS *Lusitania* was sent a direct warning about the activities of the submarine. Though the captain later admitted that there was, he did not reveal the actual wording, quoting his inability to do so under Official Secrets Legislation. There were general transmissions made to all merchant shipping which the RMS *Lusitania* was capable of receiving; however, the lack of clarity about the contents of specific messages added to conspiracy theories that emerged later. Patrick O'Sullivan maintains it was more to do with the Admiralty's reckless disregard for the ship's safety. In his intriguing book *The RMS Lusitania: Unravelling the Mysteries* he examines lesser ships that were warned directly of submarine activities in their area and were given protection by the naval authorities.[2]

For some time, the British Admiralty had been able to decipher the coded messages, sailing orders and operational instructions that were being sent from Berlin to the submarine commanders at sea. The Admiralty had information on deployment and targets of many of the U-boats, including that of the U20. Passengers, on the other hand, were unaware of the fact that the presence of the U20 was already known and that it had been targeting and sinking ships in the preceding hours as the RMS *Lusitania* sailed right into its path.

At ten minutes past two the torpedo dispatched from the U20 struck the starboard hull of the RMS *Lusitania*. There were several eyewitness accounts but like all human eyewitness accounts each one seemed slightly different from the other. Bailey and Ryan record numerous conflicting claims regarding the events immediately surrounding the attack. Some people saw the tracking wake of the torpedo coming towards the ship. Others said they saw two torpedoes and one passenger claimed to have seen three. There were claims of the submarine surfacing after the attack by one man but nobody else saw this and the U20 war records show no surfacing of the vessel.[3]

Ralf Bartzke, a student of U-boat tactics, examined available data from war records in order to put together a computerised simulation of the attack of the U20 on the ship. He took into consideration all known tactics utilised by commanders at the time and also worked

within the technological constraints of the type and operation of
the machinery that was in use in 1915.[4] In the following extract
the findings of Bartzke are presented by the RMS *Lusitania* online
resource:

As Schwieger peered into the precision optics of his attack
periscope, he had to estimate the target's speed then work out her
heading, distance, and bearing to the U-boat's bow. He estimated
her speed as being 22 knots, which was an educated guess on his
part. Target speed was usually down to an inspired estimate, but
again, data such as that gleaned by positive target identification
could help enormously. Then he saw her change course, noting
in the boat's War Diary that 'the ship turns to starboard and
takes a course to Queenstown'. By following his coded wireless
instructions from Vice-Admiral Coke, to divert RMS *Lusitania*
into Queenstown, Captain Turner was now unknowingly and
unwittingly shortening the range between his ship and the lurking
U20. To be sure his torpedo found its mark on such a fast target,
Schwieger planned to hit the ship in a fairly centralised location,
anywhere between her first and fourth funnels and preferably
around the second funnel area. Various instruments aboard the
U-Boat were used to assist in this. There was a range finding
device in the attack periscope itself, called a Stadimeter, which
was basically a split-prism range-finder. Using a double-image of
the target ship, it gave a pretty accurate range calculation up to a
maximum range of 6,000 meters. (Though at the 6, 000 meter
extremity of its range, the Stadimeter's accuracy was subject to a
10% error factor.) If certain other geometric information such as a
known masthead height or funnel height for the target could also
be factored in, even more accuracy could be obtained. Fortunately
for Schwieger, RMS *Lusitania*'s specifications were well known,
thanks to the wealth of material that had been published about
her since her completion, particularly publications such as The
Shipbuilder. (For example, RMS *Lusitania*'s masthead was 165ft
above her waterline). Contrary to popular belief, there was no
cross-wire type of target sight in a U-boat's periscope. On the

outside of the periscope's control column was a Target Bearing
Ring, which was usually read by an officer standing next to
whoever was using the periscope in the close confines of the base
of the U-boat's tower. The Target Bearing Ring gave the compass
bearing, measured in degrees, of the intended target in relation to
the U-boat's bow. All the data was then manually processed using
a slide rule and pre-determined tables to quickly calculate a firing
solution. The torpedoes travelled at different speeds, depths, and
bearing to bow – all these factors were manually programmed into
the torpedo itself. When the torpedo was ready for firing, a light
showed up for the loaded tube containing the now fully primed
torpedo. The final firing solution as predicted by Schwieger's
calculations is as follows: Target's speed estimated at 22 knots. Shot
distance; 700 metres. G6 Torpedo, optimal speed; 35 knots = 18.01
m/s (meters per second.) Torpedo running depth; 3 meters. Time
to Target after firing = 700 meters @ 18.01 m/s = 38.9 seconds.
Angle of intersection; near 90 degrees. Having run submerged
at high speed, following the calculated firing plan, U20 arrived
at the plan's pre-disposed firing point. With the boat's speed
then reduced, U20 was turned to port, into its firing position
and the designated torpedo was fired. Schwieger then relied
on a stopwatch and further periscope observations to check the
accuracy of his attack calculations. Ninety-seven years later, with
the same data fed into the simulator, Ralf's computer simulation
projected that the impact point would have been between RMS
Lusitania's second and third funnels (around Frames 161-164),
therefore amidships and pretty much where Schwieger was
aiming to hit her. However, as Schwieger observed his torpedo
hit the RMS Lusitania through his periscope, the first thing he
noticed was that the hit was much further forward of where he
planned. He immediately realised that he'd over-estimated the
speed of the RMS *Lusitania*. (The ship was in fact making just
18 knots at the time, not his estimated 22.) Then he saw and
noted the almost immediate second, larger explosion. He was at
a loss to explain this, putting it down in his War Diary to possibly
'Boilers, coal or powder?' Schwieger was not to know that by a

combination of chance and miscalculation, his shot had in fact hit the ship in the one place that would render fatal damage to her: the forward cargo hold. This is where the computer simulator Ralf used now truly comes into its own. Target's speed difference (estimated speed 22 knots – actual speed 18 knots = 4 knot difference. 4 knots = 2.06 meters per second. Hit shift = 2.06 mps for 38.9 seconds = 80.1 meters = 262.5 feet FORWARD of the original projected impact point. The control system of the G6 torpedo should have had a maximum rate of 1% possible deviation at a range of 700 metres. Maximum possible deviation was thus 7 meters (23 feet). Allowing for this possible deviation in the calculation gives us a range of the hit being the original 262.5 feet forward of the first simulated impact point +/- another possible 23 feet either way. Allowing for this possible deviation gives a final range of the hit being between 239.5 to 285.5 feet further forward of the original computer projected impact point. Those measurements, (allowing for the full scope of the possible 1% torpedo deviation) when transferred to the ship's deck plans, put the impact range anywhere between Frame 247 and possibly as far forward as, Frame 269. The mid-point of this total range is between Frames 257 and 259. These frames are all located within the RMS *Lusitania*'s forward cargo hold. Given that all relevant witness statements put the torpedo's impact behind the foremast, and that there were no survivors from the Baggage Room, (which was immediately above the projected impact area) the range is effectively narrowed to being anywhere from Frame 247 forward to Frame 257, three meters below the waterline. This computer simulation has thus confirmed the likelihood of the correctness of our original findings: that Schwieger's torpedo did indeed hit the ship in the aft end of her forward cargo hold, in the vicinity of her foremast (we originally said between frames 251 and 256) and certainly three meters below her waterline. It was also where 5,000 live artillery shells were stacked, in simple unprotected wooden crates.

Bartzke maintained that Schwieger's attack on the passing RMS *Lusitania* was opportunist and was a case of rapid-response planning. There was no time for a lengthy study of the ship's movements but it would have been common knowledge that the Cunard sister ships, the RMS *Lusitania* and the *Mauritania*, were capable of more than 26 knots at full speed. When spotted, however, the ship was making between 15 and 18.

Some passengers reported that the ship was struck forward of the bridge, others said aft. We now know that Bartzke's research narrows the area forward, not aft, to within a 23 foot margin of error. All seem to agree that there was an initial explosion that was followed by a much greater one, causing a massive plume of smoke and steam to rise high above the smokestacks. The ship immediately began to list heavily to starboard and continued ploughing through the waves in a forward motion.

Below decks, just minutes before the first explosion, men would have been going about their engine room duties, tending machinery, checking gauges for pressures in the oil, water and steam systems and stoking the boilers by shovelling huge quantities of coal into the front loading furnaces. An ever-present watch would have been kept on the 'telegraphs' which were the means by which engine movements were ordered from the bridge to the operative engine staff below. The engine room itself would have been a hot, noisy location, vibrating constantly with the circular movement of the drive-shafts transmitting rotary energy to the tail shafts which in turn imparted circular motion and power to the propellers. To generate steam, the boiler had to be kept at a sufficient temperature. Fresh water pumps, circulating oil pumps, compressors, oilers all would have contributed to the din and activity of a working environment.

In seconds after the torpedo hit there was a massive ingress of cold sea water. The horizontal level deck started to list with increasing rapidity to an angle that became an incline difficult to maintain balance on. The sound of the sea breeze was replaced with the crash of the explosions, the shattering of splintered timber, and the hissing of stream escaping from fractured pipework below. Passengers were now subjected to deafening noise, tumbling furniture and gaping

openings in decks and stairwells and the fear-stretched faces of those
try to contemplate what had happened.

The crew were ordered to deploy the lifeboats. There has been
much criticism of their efficiency. One passenger recalled:

> I am sorry to say there was certainly a lack of knowledge in the
> getting away of the lifeboats, in fact most of the boats went down
> with the ship, with the result we had no alternative but to take to
> the water. You ask if there was panic. How could it be otherwise
> with helpless women and children? I shall never blot out the sight
> from my mind.[5]

However, the launching of lifeboats is no simple procedure. In order
to deploy lifeboats a number of things have to happen. Firstly the
ropes and lines keeping the lifeboat rigidly in place in its cradle have
to be untied, uncoupled or released. Secondly, in order to launch the
boat safely, it must be raised up off the deck and moved outwards
towards the hull until it is adjacent to the deck but suspended over
the sea so that the boat is in a position to be lowered into the water.
During any time that the boat is 'suspended' it becomes vulnerable to
swinging from the movement of the ship. This inclination to swing
around while hanging freely represents the challenge of launching a
boat from a ship on the ever changing surface of the sea. This is not
the only point at which the boat becomes susceptible to damage, or
its passengers to injury.

During the period of lowering the boat towards the water the
lifting points in the boat carry its weight until it reaches the water,
where structural buoyancy of the boat causes it to float. Just before
this point is reached, however, the falls are 'let go' by a quick release
mechanism that has the effect of literally 'dropping' the boat into
the water for the last couple of inches and free the falls from the
suspension eyes. A judgement has to be made as to when to release the
falls on the way towards the water, made too early the boat will fall
from too high a distance and hit the water with an impact that could
damage or destroy the boat; made too late and the falls and release
mechanism could become fouled or caught in people or equipment

in the boat, causing injury or damage. Too late can also result in the boat being dragged along the ships side by the still attached falls. All of these considerations are complicated by the swell of the sea and the forward movement of the ship. So the successful deployment of the boats require training, skill and considerable judgement and that's not taking into account panic-stricken civilians who may be trying desperately to get aboard and get the boat into the water.

Usually when boats are being deployed the ship has to slow down to almost a stop and steered in the direction that will ensure the least amount of movement. If, like the RMS *Lusitania*, a ship is still moving speedily through the water, it makes it extremely difficult to launch a lifeboat safely. If a ship's deck is not reasonably stable, it makes it dangerous to have lifeboats suspended as they can crash into the side of the superstructure. If, like the RMS *Lusitania*, a ship was travelling at relatively fast speed and listing heavily to starboard *and* plunging deeper into the water by the head, you now have the worst possible confluence of challenges to launching a boat safely.

In their book, *The RMS Lusitania* story, Peeke, Jones and Walsh Johnson provide a graphic account of the scene on the port side of the RMS *Lusitania* during the attempts to launch the lifeboats.

At boat station number two on the port side Junior Third Officer Bestic was in charge. Standing on the after davit he was trying to keep order and explain that due to the heavy list, the boat could not be lowered. Suddenly, he heard the sound of a hammer striking the release-pin to the snubbing chain. Before the word 'NO' left his lips, the chain was freed and the five ton lifeboat laden with over fifty passengers swung inboard and crushed those standing on the boat deck against the superstructure. Unable to take the strain, the men at the davits let go the falls and no. 2 boat, plus the collapsible boat stowed behind it, slid down the deck towing a grisly collection of injured passengers and jammed under the bridge wing ...[6]

The angle of the list of the ship was such that it was impossible to release some of the securing lines that held the boats in place. Some lifeboats that were released just crashed onto the side of the hull and were irreparably damaged as a result. Nevertheless, despite very difficult circumstances, six of the eighteen cradled lifeboats were successfully launched. When one considers the ship had completely disappeared beneath the waves in just eighteen minutes, it makes the speedy dispatch of these six lifeboats all the more admirable. RMS *Titanic*, three years earlier, took a full hour to launch its first lifeboat; fewer people survived RMS *Titanic* than the RMS *Lusitania*, despite the fact that she had a lengthy two hours and forty minutes in which to fill the twenty lifeboats that she carried. With the lifeboats broken, full or unreachable on RMS *Lusitania*, many passengers found themselves flung into the sea or jumping into it to avoid being dragged to the depths when the ship went under. In Julian Thompson's *Imperial War Museum Book of the War at Sea 1914–18*,[7] letters of survivors held by the imperial war museum were published for the first time and give a sense of what some people went through:

> Mrs Phoebe Amery wrote: 'After getting in our lifeboat and after it got filled it broke to pieces throwing me into the water and I was picked up by a boat using a boathook by my hair and was clinging onto the side for 2 hours'.

Mrs Margaret Beattie was in her cabin with her husband when the torpedo struck:

> While we were on our way to the deck, my husband remembered the lifebelts and went back to the cabin for them, when we reached the middle deck we saw almost no-one, all were on the top deck where the boats were being launched. The ship at this time was very much over on her side. When we saw the sea breaking over the bows, my husband and I jumped into the water and swam for a little, and then we got hold of a plank to which we clung. After being in the water about four hours I was rescued by a trawler. My dear husband was lost, but I had great satisfaction of finding him on Saturday and seeing him laid to rest in Queenstown.

One crew member, Edward Heighway, who was in charge of one of the lifeboats, recalled the scene:

> All the decks were a mass of people when the ship suddenly threw her stern 200 feet in the air, throwing everyone headlong down among chairs, boats, seats and all sorts of loose gear. Then the ship took a plunge and went to the bottom passing me like an express train. I just got my boats two yards clear of the ship when this happened, and I am sure there were six or seven hundred people killed and taken down without a chance of saving themselves.

Many bodies were to be found washed up on beaches and shorelines of the rugged south-west coastline of Ireland, though many more were never recovered.

Despite the speed with which the ship sank, the wireless operators managed to get distress calls transmitted. These were picked up by many boats and, of course, the Admiralty in Cobh. Vessels that were already in the vicinity rushed to the aid of the stricken ship, some had even witnessed the explosions followed by the rapid sinking. Their efforts were augmented by a fleet of willing fishermen, yachtsmen and seafarers who all headed to the spot where so many had been propelled into the water. The nearest official Royal National Lifeboat Institute vessel based in Courtmacsharry was a sailing boat. Lack of wind that day delayed it reaching the ship for a number of hours. However, there were vessels closer to the disaster that sprang into action immediately. The *Wanderer* was a small fishing boat of only 21 tons that rescued 160 passengers. It towed two lifeboats towards Kinsale but before making landfall it was met by the government boat the *Flying Fish* which transferred the passengers and brought them back to Cobh.[8] The *Flying Fish* would end up playing a crucial role in the co-ordination of the rescue efforts on that fateful day.

There are some questions that do arise about the insistence on taking shocked, injured and traumatised passengers to Cobh rather than Kinsale. The *Wanderer* was only a few miles off Kinsale where they could have brought passengers to safety whereas the journey to Cobh was another 19 nautical miles. It could be argued that it was sensible as Cobh was where the regional office of Cunard were located and that there was railway and infrastructure there which Kinsale didn't have, but was it really necessary to keep the stricken passengers at sea for another few hours to take them to Cobh? It would seem that keeping those passengers at sea for a moment longer than was necessary was at least inconsiderate. It also meant keeping them in a danger zone where a submarine was known to be active. One may question whether there was a more sinister reason. Given that the Admiralty was based a Cobh, was there a desire to control the story, to shape the narrative, to retain or release whatever information to the world that would suit the war effort best? Was there forethought about what propaganda could be extracted from this tragedy? Could the dreadful loss of almost 1,200 innocent civilians be utilised from a propaganda point of view or was there an immediate need to shape a story to deflect culpability and blame from the Cunard shipping company? If so, why would the Admiralty be so interested in defending a civilian shipping group? Paddy O'Sullivan reminds us from his research that the ship had regularly carried munitions for the war effort and we know with certainty that the ship had munitions on board that day. So is it not a case that the passengers, using today's terminology, were being used as human shields?

It is a matter of great conjecture as to why passengers, on 1 May and in the days preceding the sailing of the ship from New York, were not aware of the deadly threat posed by the exclusion zone patrolled by the German Navy submarine fleet. Would anybody in their right mind set out on a journey if they knew that it would end in death or destruction? If not, is it reasonable to consider that they were either ill-informed or unrealistically re-assured? It is very clear that many passengers on the ship up to 2.10 p.m. that day were blissfully unaware that by 2.30 p.m. they would have experienced the most horrific consequences of a ship being struck and the consequent mangle of twisted steel, smoke and steam that would end the lives of so many innocent fellow passengers. Who bears responsibility for the lack of information regarding the real dangers of trans-Atlantic travel at the time? Should the Cunard Company not have issued stronger warnings to their passengers about the threat? How many passengers would have embarked if they had been told that the ship was loaded with munitions?

HMS *Juno*

While the whole maelstrom of death and destruction was unfolding around the RMS *Lusitania* and its passengers, another scenario was being played out that leaves questions unanswered to this day. The movements of HMS *Juno* led to one of the early conspiracy theories that emerged amid the tragic aftermath of the death of so many civilians. Official explanations, such as they are, still leave uncomfortable questions. HMS *Juno* was part of a group of five light cruisers mentioned in chapter 2 that formed the operationally entitled 'Cruiser Force E'. The five ships were stationed in and around the southern approaches to the Irish Sea. Since 19 February 1915 this was an area that was included in the German designated warzone that had been announced by the German government on 4 February. These ships, despite their age, were warships. They had been designed and built with conflict in mind. They were crewed by Royal Naval personnel and reservists. They were armed with heavy 6-inch guns. One must assume they were in position as a deterrent to the threat of submarine attack and that they were there as a means of protection for the merchant ships using the busy shipping lanes to Liverpool and other ports on the east coast of Great Britain. They were there to keep the access open to the Irish Sea and, as previously stated, to provide 'cover to liners, cargo carriers and tramp steamers'.[9] Why then was RMS *Juno* instructed to flee a danger zone after the attack?

On the morning of 7 May 1915, when RMS *Lusitania* had entered the warzone, HMS *Juno* was operational off the south coast of Ireland. From midnight up until 2 p.m. that day she was steaming in an east to west direction along the coastline. Captain Turner, according to some authors, may have been expecting a naval escort through the zone from a navy ship but never got it.

An examination of the log book for that day on HMS *Juno* reveals detailed information on the ship's movements.[10] She had been hampered by thick fog while steaming through the night. Having reduced speed down to 6 knots at one stage, she increased and made steady progress at 12 knots between 4 a.m. and 8 a.m. At 8 a.m., still travelling in a westerly direction, the ship increased her speed to 15 knots and began to adopt a zigzagging course towards Cobh. At this stage that the Admiralty were aware of the submarine activity off the south coast of Ireland and the attacks that had occurred the day before. RMS *Lusitania* had also received a general warning that there was submarine activity in the vicinity. Why then was HMS *Juno* going to Cobh? Should she not have been on her way to escort the RMS *Lusitania*, or at least provide a deterring presence? By midday HMS *Juno* was off the Daunt Rock, which is situated in the approaches to Cork Harbour. She steamed in the entrance to the harbour, passing Roche's Point Lighthouse at 1.45 p.m., and began the half-hour journey that would take her to Cobh Roads, the area of the natural channel that runs immediately in front of the waterfront of Cobh. At 2.15 p.m., six minutes after the torpedo had struck RMS *Lusitania* only 20 miles away, HMS *Juno* was approaching mooring buoy number 2 off Cobh. At 2.30 p.m. the ship was secured to the buoy and fully moored. RMS *Lusitania* was already beneath the waves at this point with hundreds of men, women and children already dead, the remainder trashing around in the sea, clinging to broken furniture and boats in a bid for survival.

At 3 p.m. HMS *Juno* made ready for sea again and detached herself from the mooring for departure. The deployment at this point of a naval vessel could have been for any number of reasons; however, it seems certain that it had to do with RMS *Lusitania* and the assigned task of the Light Cruiser Squadron at that time in that part of the world. It would be reasonable to suggest any of the following:

- HMS *Juno* was instructed to undertake a rescue operation for the passengers of RMS *Lusitania*, many of whom are injured, clinging to life or dying in the water.

- HMS *Juno* was deployed to hunt down the perpetrator of the attack so that it may not be in a position to attack another vessel.
- HMS *Juno* was ordered to take tactical command of the rescue operation and co-ordinate the many smaller vessels that were already making their way towards the scene of the tragedy.
- HMS *Juno* was dispatched to provide an escort for those that were picking up passengers, thus protecting them from further attack from a submarine.
- The captain of HMS *Juno* became aware of the sinking of the RMS *Lusitania* and decided to let go the mooring and proceed to sea of his own volition.
- Vice-Admiral Coke issued a sailing order to HMS *Juno* to make due haste to the scene of the sinking.

Any one of these scenarios could have been reasonably assumed by anyone watching the naval ship steam away from the buoy in the direction of the harbour entrance had they known just what had happened in the waters off the Old Head of Kinsale. The ship steamed out of the harbour from Cobh Roads at a speed of 8 knots. She passed Roche's Point outward bound at 3.40 p.m. and cleared the harbour entrance. HMS *Juno* was now well positioned to render assistance to the stricken passengers of RMS *Lusitania*. By this time, less than 18 miles away, frantic efforts were being made to rescue people from the water. HMS *Juno*, with a listed top speed of 19 knots, had already be doing 16 knots steadily earlier that morning, would have reached the site of the sunken RMS *Lusitania* in about one hour or a little over it. At this crucial juncture, in the minutes and hours immediately following the sinking, time was of the essence. The seawater was not freezing as had been the case in the *Titanic* tragedy three years before. (On that occasion the passengers entering the water had only about fifteen minutes before hypothermia set in. Most *Titanic* passengers died from exposure and froze to death.) In the case of RMS *Lusitania*, the water was warmer, having been recorded that morning at 51°F. While this temperature could hardly be described as warm, it did give passengers more time before the worst effects of hypothermia would begin to set in. For these reasons, time was absolutely critical.

Incredibly, HMS *Juno*, having left the precincts of Cork Harbour in the direction of the Old Head of Kinsale, after just ten minutes outward bound, completed a 180 degree turn to steam straight back into the harbour to Cobh. By 4.35 p.m. she was again secured safely to number 2 buoy at Cobh Roads. People were still dying in the water off Kinsale and smaller boats were still making their way to the scene of the disaster. One of them, the *Woodnut*, is noted in the log of HMS *Juno* as passing the moored naval vessel to make its way out to try and find more survivors. On board the naval ship the off-duty watch was granted leave to go ashore.

There have been many questions asked over the years about the actions of HMS *Juno* that day. Conspiracy theories have blossomed around it. While speculation isn't always a good thing, in the absence of reasonable explanations it is inevitable. Let the reader consider the facts as they are known.

HMS *Juno* was a fighting ship. She was a military vessel. She was deployed in a certain area to undertake a certain task. She was under the tactical command of the Admiralty who were represented in Cobh by the Queenstown Command based in Admiralty House there. A naval ship is not a leisure craft, it does not exist for the pleasure of its crew, and it is not a commercial vessel in pursuit of trade. A naval ship acts in the interests of and at the direction of its government. A ship will return to port and abort a mission only if it is instructed to do so or if it has become incapacitated to such an extent that it cannot complete its mission. Sufficient to say, this particular fighting ship did not return to Cobh of its own volition. It was not incapacitated by mechanical failure or human error. There was no mutiny on board. They were not inhibited in their journey by bad weather. The logbook for the day notes when the ship returns to her mooring at number 2 buoy that she has been 'made fast as req'. In naval terminology this means 'as requested', 'as required' or 'as requisite'. From this it is evident that the ship's company were carrying out orders from a higher authority. The question arises as to why a naval vessel would be ordered back;

why a naval vessel would knowingly leave the scene of such a great human tragedy.

One unsubstantiated local belief that was still in circulation in Cobh when the author first took an interest in these matters in the 1970s was that the captain of HMS *Juno*, soon after he moored at buoy number 2, had heard of the attack off the Old Head of Kinsale. The story goes that he decided to proceed to sea immediately and sought the requisite permission when he was already under way. In the author's time in service in the Irish Navy there was a common practice at least in the 1970s and 1980s that a ship would receive its sailing order before patrol from the highest naval authority at Naval General Headquarters, at that time in based in Dublin. In spite of having the specific orders from the senior Naval Officer in the country, to embark on a certain mission and leave the Naval Base at a specific time on a specific date, it was common practice, as a matter of courtesy, to seek the permission of the Senior Officer on the Naval Base to slip and proceed in compliance with orders. The interesting practice here was that this permission was often sought after the ship had left the base and was already proceeding down the harbour. In fact, the old Aldis Lamps used for Morse coded messages were traditionally used for that particular signal. One of the persistent beliefs that remained in Cobh for many years after the tragedy of the RMS *Lusitania* was that HMS *Juno* unmoored herself and steamed out the harbour to give aid to the RMS *Lusitania* seeking permission to proceed as she went, but the signal that came back was 'not granted'.

Another theory suggests that when he became aware of the sinking of the RMS *Lusitania* and the huge implications for loss of life, Vice-Admiral Coke ordered HMS *Juno* to go back to sea to render assistance. He then advised the Admiralty in London after he had ordered the ship to sea and it was the Admiralty, under First Sea Lord Fisher and First Lord of the Admiralty Winston Churchill, that countermanded his decision and instructed he order the *Juno* back to Cobh.

It is known that the ship did not have any mechanical problems to force her to return. It is known that she had embarked on a voyage to the area where the ship was attacked. It is known that while the manoeuvrability of the larger ship would not be as responsive as the smaller vessels attending the scene of the sinking it would have been a great asset, physically and psychologically in the rescue operation. It is known that the crew were at all times compliant with their orders. What is not known is why the ship was called back.

It has been argued by many that the thinking at the time by the Admiralty was that the smaller vessels were better equipped to pick up the passengers from the water. But a naval ship like HMS *Juno*, of 5,500 tons, with a usual crew capacity of 450 men, could surely contribute enormously to the saving of lives. Little fishing boats were picking up people from the water in their dozens and packing them onto cramped deck spaces with the dogged intention of saving as many as was humanely possible. These boats did so without the protection of being armed. A submarine could have resurfaced at any time to threaten them but they worked on relentlessly. HMS *Juno* was armed with eleven 6-inch guns and other smaller but lethal armaments. It could have provided that protection.

Some have suggested that the sinking of HMS *Aboukir*, HMS *Cressy* and HMS *Hogue* the previous September by a submarine caused a reluctance to risk another vessel of the same type. The Admiralty didn't want to risk the loss of a fighting ship to a submarine that might be lying in wait. The incident, however, was at an early stage in the war and the element of surprise coupled with the Royal Navy's lack of experience in engaging with hostile submarines were a distinct disadvantage at that time. Experience since then meant they were in a much better position to ward off such attacks. In addition, the Admiralty by May 1915 had the massive intelligence advantage of knowing the intended movements of submarines, having been in possession of German Naval communication codes for some time.

Writers and apologists for the actions of HMS *Juno* have persistently argued that the ship was unsuitable for service against submarines. Why? She was twice as fast, more heavily armed and had a crew of hundreds to keep a watchful eye on the surface of the ocean for the tell-tale periscope of submarines and the conning towers that would appear at regular intervals when the submarines had to surface. The day before the sinking of the RMS *Lusitania*, the U20 crossed paths with HMS *Juno* but was unable to engage with her because of her superior speed.[11] In addition to the ship's advantage in speed, the submarine would have been inhibited in its ability to surface anywhere near the ship as any one of eleven 6-inch guns could be trained on a surface target that presented itself such as a conning tower. The 6-inch guns generally had a range well in excess of 5,000 yards. The speed of HMS *Juno* together with her firepower made her a formidable foe against a submarine that may have to expose itself on the surface, particularly if it was out of torpedo range.

An interesting narrative emerged in Cobh years later, and still remains there to this day, that the *Juno* was so old and obsolete that the Royal Navy scrapped her immediately after the incident. Again there is no foundation to this myth. The ship was in service until it was sold in 1920 having been on station for the Royal Navy in Persian Gulf and the East Indies from July of 1914.[12]

But even if the description of HMS *Juno* as an aging unsuitable craft were valid, why have it and four other ships of that design deployed in this area in the first place? Why was the 11th Squadron of Light Cruisers deployed in the area at all if they couldn't risk being in the presence of submarines? If they were not operationally fit to engage with a submarine, why were the weapons and armaments not deployed to other vessels? Trawlers, yachts and hundreds of non-threatening craft were already being used in an offensive role off the coast of Great Britain to engage, fire on and, where possible, sink submarines. Also, if there was such a fear and an intention not to engage with the submarine, why initially send HMS *Juno* to sea after the RMS *Lusitania* had been struck?

A more sinister explanation for the Juno's order to return is plausible. In their book on the RMS *Lusitania*, Peeke, Jones and Walsh-Johnson explain that Winston Churchill was hoping for a merchant ship to become a casualty of a submarine attack, they instance a letter from Churchill to Walter Runciman who was the President of the Board of Trade in which he writes: '… it is most important to attract neutral shipping to our shores, in the hope especially embroiling the US with Germany ... for our part we want the traffic the more of it the better and if some of it gets into trouble, better still.'[13]

It is evident that in the British Government and the War Department there was a great desire to have the United States join the war on their side. Armies had become bogged down on the green fields of the European continent as they shelled each other from trench to trench and foxhole to foxhole. It cannot have escaped the attention of those involved in diplomacy that the sinking of the RMS *Lusitania* with its 189 American citizens on board may become a factor in persuading the US to enter the war. President Wilson, just twelve weeks earlier, had responded to the German warnings about the imposition of and exclusion zone that they would be 'held strictly to account' if the rights of American citizens were compromised by their actions. Did Winston Churchill now see that the RMS *Lusitania* tragedy may have a positive effect in the international balance of power?

A lot of speculation and conspiracies theories emerged after the sinking, some of which gained more ground than others. It was even suggested that Winston Churchill orchestrated the sinking of the RMS *Lusitania*. Could he have directly influenced the sailing schedule of Cunard to leave New York at a specific time, proceed at a certain speed, arrive at a certain point in the vastness of the sea to coincide with a the arrival of a particular submarine in the same space and time? Would he have then had the certainty that the ship could be struck at a particular angle in a particular point of the hull to maximise damage? This seems a most unlikely scenario, affording unrealistic powers of influence and organisation not just of the accurate positioning of the ship at sea but also of a German submarine, even if the Admiralty were aware of the movements of all German submarines in the area at the time.

However, one scenario deserves consideration. It was a matter of common belief that Churchill, the War Department and the British Government all desired the participation of the United States in the war. When the initial horror of the loss of the ship was first reported, would the thought that this tragedy may encourage the United States into the war have entered the heads of anybody who had previously wished them to go to war? Was it possible that, since the ship had already been sunk, certain actions were taken or not taken to maximise the loss of life in order to maximise the impact on the American position of neutrality? Was the cessation of the outward voyage of a Royal Naval vessel ordered with the intention of reducing the numbers that could be saved from the RMS *Lusitania*?

Is it possible that the loss of an increased number of lives in the tragedy was seen as a reasonable sacrifice to make in the efforts to avert the killing of millions. A prolonged conflict was likely to sap the lifeblood out of Great Britain, economically and humanely. Would an affronted United States help alleviate the massive pressure Great Britain was experiencing in trying to execute the war? And would the loss of an increased number of American lives help persuade America to enter the war and effect its outcome? This possible motivation is worthy of consideration. Despite the fact that the US was ill-prepared for a conflict in Europe, there was a desire in Great Britain to have her involved. This scenario may seem callous but there are many examples in history of one group being sacrificed for the greater good and survival. Was it a case that 1,200 dead would be a price to pay to save millions of others?

If such beliefs were there at the time were they not reasonable? As it transpired the sinking of the RMS *Lusitania* did not bring America into the war, so if that was the motivation that prompted the recall of HMS *Juno*, it was a gamble and a sacrifice that did not pay off. There was no justification whatsoever for HMS *Juno* being recalled when she was only one hour from the hundreds of passengers in the water that day.

9

Human Tragedy

The full range of human tragedy that followed the sinking of the RMS *Lusitania* is difficult to comprehend from the reading of a book. Real people found themselves witnessing horrific events and literally saw men, women and children lose their lives around them in a variety of ways. Some were atomised by the massive explosion that took place on board, fuelled by the simultaneous ignition of an illegal substance. Whether the substance was explosives for use in munitions or whether it was more industrial than military, either way, ships were prohibited by US legislation from carrying any explosive materials on board that would threaten the life of passengers.

The townspeople of Cobh were also traumatised by the events that unfolded. Survivors and those not so lucky were brought ashore to the back of the Cunard Company building and the pier. Fishermen were reported to have been compelled to make life and death decisions and according to one of Cobh's local historians, John Hennessy, they had to push people away from their boat lest it be overcrowded and capsized. Michael Cotter, who was in his eighties in the 1960s, had been a local fisherman and part of the volunteer crew of the Cobh lifeboat which was stationed at the eastern end of the town. Cotter told John that it got so bad that they had to use a knife to release the fingers of drowning passengers who were causing the little fishing boat to roll dangerously. His recollections of the drowning passengers that he could not help remained with Cotter for the rest of his life.[1]

Today Cobh lifeboat station is long gone but the building maintains a maritime link in that it is in use as a Sea Scout hall.

Survivors in Cobh. (Courtesy *Cork Examiner*)

Ironically only yards away, a Titanic Memorial Garden was unveiled in 2014 to commemorate the lost passengers of the *Titanic*. Little do people know as they enter the garden a small nondescript building by the seashore was the launching point of a little boat in which ordinary local men played a heroic and difficult role in trying to reduce the loss of life resulting from the attack on the RMS *Lusitania*.

On the evening of the sinking and in the days following, as the little fishing boats and trawlers came ashore with their grisly cargoes, coffins were made ready for the dead. The coffins were stacked up beneath the canopy at the back of the Cunard Company offices. At time of writing, the Cunard Company have long since departed but the original building and indeed the canopy itself are still there, chilling reminders of the great human tragedy that unfolded in May of 1915. There were so many caskets needed that funeral directors as far away as the city of Cork were engaged to build them. The bodies were laid out in a number of different buildings that acted as temporary mortuaries in the town. These included the nearby White Star Line/America Line building, the Cunard office, the Port Customs building and occasionally, very temporary buildings elsewhere. Numerous descriptions in journals and newspapers in the days following give graphic accounts of distraught relatives shuffling from one place to another looking for their loved ones. The cool and cavernous mail room of the White Star Line became a temporary area where the dead were laid out and the process of trying to identify them could begin. One local man posed for a photograph of him tenderly holding the body of a deceased child in his arms in the hope that the little one could be recognised in a British or American Newspaper. To that point no one had come forward to identify and claim her.

The survivors were accommodated in the many local hotels, rooming houses and guest house that were situated along the main street of the town. Some of the houses in close proximity to the Cunard office were converted into first aid stations where surviving passengers with injuries or shock trauma were treated. The Rob Roy Hotel in the town's second square and the Queens Hotel (known in 2014 as the Commodore Hotel) were both utilised for passenger's

Extra coffins brought to Cobh. (Courtesy *Cork Examiner*)

accommodation. In the case of the Commodore it became almost like a hospital. Local rumour had it that the owners of the building were of German extraction and, on hearing of the RMS *Lusitania* attack, they hid themselves in the cellars of the great building until any protests had passed. An early original sketched depiction of RMS *Lusitania* still remains over one of the hotels original arch doorways near the entrance today. The owners of the hotel are in possession of a letter that was sent by the self-appointed matron of the temporary

The arched doorway with the *Lusitania* Mural. (Commodore Hotel Cobh)

'hospital'. She had come to Cobh from South Africa and in the letter she remarks about coming to Cobh for a rest from the incessant reporting and conflict gripping England during the Great War. Her letter expresses irony that the First World War and all its terrible consequences had come to the peaceful harbour while she was there.

Within days passengers who were fit and well were transported by rail to Dublin to then cross the Irish Sea, back to England. Others stayed on in the forlorn diminishing hope that their loved ones might be found. The railway station in 2014 has had a large part of it converted into an interactive museum. The theme of the exhibit is centred on emigration but also covers the maritime tradition of Cork harbour. There are sections on the Royal Naval presence, the American Navy's arrival during the First World War and a little area dealing with the RMS *Lusitania* and *Titanic* tragedies. An old movie reel reflecting the robust opinions of the day can be played by the touch of a button.

Back in 1915 the nearby Old Church cemetery was made ready for the large number of graves that had to be prepared. The funeral processions that took place in the little town of Cobh imposed a solemn cloud of mourning over the town for several days. Hundreds of silent onlookers lined the streets and sloping hill from the town to the graveyard. Horse-drawn carriages carrying not one but many coffins were used to transport the dead from the temporary mortuaries in the town to the cemetery. Contingents of the local serving military personnel were given the onerous task of digging three very large mass graves. The victims were separated in death by denomination. Catholics went into one and Protestants into the other two. The Bishop of Cloyne officiated over the funeral of those known to be and those thought to be Catholic and likewise the Church of Ireland Bishop officiated over the Protestant believers. In addition to the three mass graves there were over twenty-five individual plots. Most of which can still be clearly seen today. One of the headstones marks the grave of a young 4-year-old boy whose name was Scott Witherbee Junior. The inscription embodies the tragedy and outrage felt by his loved ones that a child so young

Mass burial in Cobh. (Courtesy *Cork Examiner*)

could be taken so unexpectedly and suddenly. It reads, 'A victim of the Lusitania crime, foully murdered by Germany'.

Many visitors still go to the cemetery today where information boards and plaques explain the significance of the site. One local man, Jack Gilmartin, made a lifetime study of those who lie buried in the cemetery because in addition to the RMS *Lusitania* victims there are many military graves of those lost in service during the First World War. Soldiers, sailors and civilians including a man named Parslow who was awarded the Victoria Cross. All are buried side by side under the simple but distinctive headstones that mark service during the war. Not far from them another plot bears the bodies of Irish volunteers who died during the War of Independence in an ambush conducted by serving British military personnel. They all lie equal in peace.

From the time of the sinking it had been a matter of discussion among local people that Cobh should erect a fitting memorial to mark the tragedy of the extent of the loss of life. In the final year of his studies Kevin McCarthy, a young Cobh resident and student of University College Cork, researched and wrote a paper on the erection of the memorial in the town.[2] McCarthy examined the minuted meetings of Cobh Urban District Council where discussion and often argument arose about the type and fitting location of a monument for the town. An American committee was also formed and fundraising began. Before long it became known that Jerome Connor was to be selected as the sculptor. A protracted and difficult relationship began during which there would be inordinate delays, threats of withdrawal and even legal cases and correspondence before the memorial was finally erected. Today that memorial holds a prominent position in one of the main town squares. Casement Square is a beautiful example of Georgian Architecture and style. It consists of an arched market house building on one end and on either side a row of the original three-storey buildings from the early 1800s. One side curves gracefully round to the esplanade at Westbourne. Centre stage, at the open end of the square, the RMS Lusitania Peace Memorial is made up of a circular stepped plinth surrounding the main monument. It is in two sections. The upper half depicts the Angel of Peace. The angel stands on a sword in a symbolic gesture to end world conflict. The sculptor was formed using the 'lost wax process' which enables a real object such as a face to be cast initially in wax which is placed into casting sand and then drained to allow the pouring of metal where the was cast once was. The effect is to create an image from a real face. Beneath the feet of the angel there is an Irish language inscription which reads '*Síocháin in Anim Dé*' ('Peace in God's Name'). The lower half of the statue depicts two lifesize, almost dishevelled fishermen. The strain and fatigue is captured magnificently in their harrowed faces. They also carry an inscription beneath their feet. It is in Latin and announces, '*Laborare est Orare*' ('To Work is to Pray'). This seems a fitting sentiment since it was the great effort and bravery of ordinary fishermen who managed to save over 760 passengers and crew from the sea. A plaque on the pavement in front of the memorial records the loss of 1,198 people. This figure does not take account of the three gentlemen reported to have been detained on the ship soon after she left from New York on suspicion of espionage.

A former Presbyterian Church overlooking the harbour has housed the Cobh local civic and maritime museum since the 1970s. This little building, located on the edge of the town centre, is a treasure trove of local artefacts, many with a maritime connection. There is a deckchair gifted to the museum that is reputed to have been washed up on the shore near where RMS *Lusitania* sunk. There is a log book on display that recorded the narrative of the harbour master about the sinking of the RMS *Lusitania*:

'Huns Awful Crime'
RMS *Lusitania* torpedoed off Cork Harbour.
One of the most appalling crimes in history was perpetrated off the Cork Coast yesterday. About 2 in the afternoon in beautiful weather the Cunard Liner RMS *Lusitania* 9145 tons reg. 32,000 gross which left New York last Saturday was passing the coast on her way to Liverpool, when a few miles off the Old Head while the passengers were at lunch a torpedo was fired from a sub. No warning whatever was given. The great ship was struck near the 2nd funnel and at once began to sink by the head. A 2nd and some say a 3rd torpedo struck the ship. In a very few minutes the liner began to fall over on her side rendering the lowering of the lifeboats at one side impossible. In about 20 minutes of the first torpedo having struck her the RMS *Lusitania* had disappeared beneath the waters.

Lifeboat ration. (Courtesy Cobh Museum)

In a back room, in a temperature- and humidity-controlled cabinet, a treasured artefact of the RMS *Lusitania* tragedy is respectfully preserved. At that time and to this day lifeboats always carry some kind of emergency rations and essentials for survival. In the past these often included oat-like biscuits that may have not been noted for their taste but nevertheless would have provided a minimal amount of nutrition to help lifeboat victims survive. Cobh Museum has such a biscuit. It came from a lifeboat on the RMS *Lusitania* and was gifted to the museum by a local family who maintained that it was recovered by a local British service man, J. Law, stationed at Templebreedy which was a defensive firing position overlooking Cork Harbour's entrance. Law, who was involved in the recovery and rescue operation following the sinking of the ship, wrote on the biscuit at the time, inscribing at the centre: 'A relic of the RMS *Lusitania* taken out of one of her boats. Sunday 9 May 1915 by J. Law Templebreedy'. Around the periphery of the biscuit it reads: 'SS Lusitania sunk by a German submarine off the "Old Head of Kinsale" Friday May 7th 1915'. On the reverse side in what looks like different handwriting: 'Keep this as a souvenir'.

10

American Neutrality

It would appear that while most people are aware of the fact that America played an important role in the war, many seem unaware of both the short period of her involvement and the background to her remaining outside of the conflict for more than half of its duration. The United States of America had no intention of entering the war when it started. They had no hand or act or part in its origin. The president of the day not only had grave reservations about war as a means of settling any dispute but also believed he had a mandate from the American people to keep them out of the conflict. He had a deep abhorrence himself for war; however, that was not his only consideration in keeping the United States out of the conflict for as long as he did. President Wilson perceived the whole business of a European conflict as a matter for serious consideration in maintaining the integrity of the country which he led.

Woodrow Wilson was born on 28 December 1856. He was elected as President of the United States of America in March 1913 and served until March 1921. It was during his tenure of office that American policy towards the First World War was formulated. He was a member of the Democratic Party. He was a well-educated man graduating from Princeton (then called the College of New Jersey) and completing a PhD in political science from John Hopkins University. He became a professor of history from 1888 and later a professor of political science. In 1902 he was appointed President of the University. Wilson was a man that knew his own country's history – he had written on the subject – and he had a sense of America's place in the world and how it should react to issues of global significance.

Some British observers in the years following the sinking of the RMS *Lusitania* suggested Wilson's stance on neutrality was down to indecision and a dilemma:

> … it was difficult for President Wilson to know how he should act for the good of his country. Whilst one party urged him to enter the war against the British blockade, and another body of opinion was for instantly coming in against Germany's submarine blockade, yet a third section insisted on traditional aloofness from European troubles.[1]

This view suggests that he did not know what position to take in the war because of the divergent views of his constituents in the US. This was not the case. President Wilson had very specific views on the position that the United States should adopt during the war. He had deeply-held principled views about maintaining the integrity of American sovereignty. Many scholars have written on the subject. Robert Tucker's work examines Wilson's thinking in detail and reveals a robust, considered position on neutrality based on diplomatic endeavours to improve international relations and to position war as a futile and destructive endeavour.[2] The President also felt from the beginning that by entering the war, the US would lose any capacity to have a meaningful influence of any settlement that would inevitably come after the war. It was felt that a feature of neutrality would be to leave the country in a much stronger position to further American interests in whatever the post-war world would be. The policy pursued was supposedly twofold: on one hand to continually endeavour to preserve peace and on the other to preserve the neutral rights of the US. In defending the rights of being a neutral country they were also endeavouring to preserve the rights of other neutrals. From the outset of the war American foreign policy as advocated by the President was not to just act as neutrals but to think as neutrals too. He was a man that was not swayed easily and was often described as being like a judicial figure, weighing up evidence of advisors or events and coming very much to his own decisions.

> Wilson was like a judge sitting in court. He received the evidence on fact, listened to expert witnesses and to the respectful submissions of counsel, reserved judgement, and then gave his decision. After that the court was closed. If a judge can be said to be advised by counsel and witnesses - for this is what the process described by Lansing and Tumulty amount to - then Wilson took advice. But he never took advice in the sense of preferring somebody else's judgement to his own.[3]

Large numbers of the population of the United States would have felt sympathetic towards the countries of their origin. These included belligerents and neutral alike so not surprisingly criticisms and/or sympathies varied enormously among the general population and moved from one position to another as events unfolded and the war went on.

There were numerous elements to the position of neutrality. They included economic, philosophical and pragmatic arguments that could be made to keep the US at a distance from causes and consequences of the warring parties of other nations. It was in his people's interest to be in a position to continue to conduct business with all participants in the conflict. Vital trade between Europe and the US contributed enormously to the economic fabric of the US economy and the wellbeing of its citizens. If the United States entered the war for no other reason than it could, there were massive implications to trade. One side-effect of being at war would be the suspension of normal trade relations. Any group of countries forming an alliance consisted of millions of citizens. Thus there were thousands of potential markets and hundreds of opportunities for the sale of produce and goods. In the multimillion-citizen-sized markets of a group of allied countries such as were involved in the conflict in Europe, aligning oneself with one side or the other could mean a loss of immeasurable income and reduced employment on the home front. Being at war also meant inevitable shortages arising in all sorts of goods in the countries that were in conflict. Eager American manufactures could step in to fill the gap and position themselves as replacement suppliers to those markets that were suffering shortages as a result of the war. The US in the first half of the war traded with all sides and Britain's blockades of German ports and the North Sea was a pressing concern for America at the time. Employment and the flowing of market product into the European cities and ports would have been a major consideration in shaping how the US would approach the idea of conflict with another country. From a pragmatic point of view, the President had to consider the impact on the US should either the Allies or the Germans be victorious. Tucker suggests that whatever Wilson's public position he would have believed that a British victory would have less negative consequences for the United States. But taking a position of pure neutrality one could not be seen to favour one side over the other. If, for example, the German side should emerge victorious from the war it would be far more beneficial to the US in a post-conflict situation not to have been seen to be favouring one side over the other.

From a moral standpoint it was difficult for America to really understand what the conflict was about other than to defeat a rival. There was certainly an attitude in the US that Europeans constantly engaged in shifting alliances, expansionism and oppression of one people over another. Migration to the United States of millions of people over the years was driven in many instances by matters such as conflict and economic impoverishment. In many cases, the systems of government, including those involving a monarchy, did not include equal division of wealth or opportunity. Many European societies were structured to favour the ruling classes at the expense of those in the lower echelons of the social strata. The last thing America needed was to be allied to any particular country or Royal family that would change and shift alliances on the basis of a family argument or an ancient call of one particular tract of land over another.

In addressing Congress just before America's eventual entry into the war the president of the US remarked:

> … We have no quarrel with the German people. We have no feeling towards them but one of sympathy and friendship. It was not upon their impulse that their government acted in entering the war. It was not with their previous knowledge or approval. It was a war determined upon as wars used to be in the old unhappy days when peoples were nowhere consulted by their rulers and wars were provoked and waged in the interest of dynasties or little groups of ambitious men who were accustomed to use their fellow men as pawns and tools.[4]

The war was seen by President Woodrow Wilson as a fight for power between groups of nations. Robert Tucker argues that Wilson could see no compelling moral significance on either side for the outbreak of the war, although he suggests the sinking of the RMS *Lusitania* brought the US and Germany to the brink of war.[5] A position of neutrality was of benefit to the US from a number of perspectives. Financially it could trade with all belligerents and accrue enormous economic benefit, strategically it could end up being a powerbroker in a world order weakened by the conflict, morally it could claim that it was not seen to take sides, remaining available to 'lead' others out of war and politically it was important that any decision to go to war would be taken in the sole interests of the American people. This protected and strengthened the sovereignty of the country as a whole. The argument went that if a country was compelled to enter a conflict on the whims of another, it had lost its own independence. In the next major European conflict to emerge, the Second World War, Ireland took the same strategic view as America had in 1914 and insisted that neutrality was linked to sovereignty and a true feature of real independence. And so, the position of the United States for most of the war was one of neutrality. Very soon after the conflict started they were calling for the rights of neutral countries to be respected and the implementation of defined rules governing the conduct of war, as discussed in Chapter 5.

In 1909, several years before the war, ten naval powers from around the world were invited to London to draw up a declaration outlining agreed rules for naval blockades and treatment of belligerent and neutral vessels during time of war. Although this treaty was not ratified, within days of the outbreak of the First World War, the United States Government was appealing for all belligerents to adopt the 'Declaration of London'. The British Government, who had rejected the original declaration, refused. President Wilson and the American Government had much to fear about Britain's blockade in the North Sea. Massive amounts of legitimate trade resulted in hundreds of American cargo vessels entering and leaving German ports. The Declaration of London provided that such ships should have been given free passage. Britain's total control of access to and from the North Sea and of Germany was in breach of its own (unratified) declaration. This and the fact that non-participating neutral countries were being affected enabled others to claim that Britain's blockade was illegal. Britain argued that this was not the case as ships could pass freely but on condition that they would subject themselves to inspection by British Naval ships before proceeding. This argument had a number of problems. Firstly it could be argued that no country had any rights whatsoever in the open sea to stop, detain or search a ship from a state with whom it was not at war. Secondly any ship not allowing themselves be searched did not technically have free passage. A series of strategically placed minefields made safe navigation impossible into the North Sea unless one had a Royal Naval escort that would lead a ship safely through the lethal obstruction. This would be promised of course but only if the ship subjected itself to a search. It was believed by many, including President Wilson, that Britain was in breach of general international law in pursuing this practice. Wilson would never accept the legality of Britain's so called 'pseudo-blockade' and in 1916 persuaded congress to grant him powers to prohibit loans to Britain and impose embargoes on the country if those type of retaliatory measures became necessary. The fact that these were not used was, according to Seymour, because:

any practicable measures designed to enforce our interpretation of international law would have ruined the interests they meant to safeguard. By our formal protests we protected our ultimate property rights and built up a case for future damages to be proved before an international tribunal.[6]

Actions to impose embargoes and prohibit loans are powerful diplomatic moves that indicate a deterioration of international relations. Embargoes are the diplomatic equivalent on non-acceptance of a government's policy or actions. Such measures often precipitate conflict although most scholars agree that, despite strained relations on this issue, actual conflict between the US and Great Britain would be highly unlikely. And so the United States was more discommoded by British actions at sea during the first year of the war than by any German initiatives. On paper at least America had less of a grievance with Germany than it had with Britain. Numerous informal briefings were made by the United States Government to the British Government regarding the 'blockade' of the North Sea and the impact on legitimate American commercial trade. The humiliation of having American ships stopped and searched by another sovereign power was not easily accepted. It may or may not have resulted in a deeper deterioration of relations. While the operation of the blockade wounded American pride, certain materials and cargoes still made it to their destination and even if they didn't, the ships carrying them were not sunk. Later, German actions that resulted in American loss of life were to test relations in a far deeper way between the US and Germany than any blockade had done previously between the US and Britain.

Once the submarine exclusion zone was announced by Germany on 4 February 1915, materials and goods were now in danger of being destroyed or lost. In the same way that the US had sent a note of protest to Britain about the injustice and possible illegality of the blockades, they now sent a note of protest to Germany about the imposition of a declared warzone around Britain and Ireland and the inherent threat to vessels that entered it. Six days after the German declaration, in almost subservient language, the US protest note opens by outlining what is deemed to be the duty of the administration to '… call the attention of the Imperial government, with sincere respect and the most friendly sentiments but very candidly and earnestly, to the very serious possibilities of the course of action apparently contemplated.'[7] It then advised the German Government of the critical situation in the two countries relations that might arise if an American ship were to be destroyed or an American life lost. The note was very specific in outlining what the United States believed was the only approach that could be taken in respect of neutral ships, i.e. that engagement was limited to visit and search. Interestingly the note distinguishes between visit and search on the high seas and a blockade. Suggesting that visit and search is a right of the belligerent once a blockade has not been imposed and reminding Germany that they had not done so. The note stated that declaring the right to attack any ship on the high seas without determining its belligerent nationality and contraband nature of its cargo would be an act '… unprecedented in Naval warfare …'[8] It also rejected the excuse by Germany in its declaration that it could not distinguish between neutral and belligerent ships because of the practice of British ships misusing flags of neutral countries. Britain's use of neutral flags to deflect the attention of German submarines had been witnessed by many passengers and crews on the Atlantic route. Quoting one of the fundamental bedrocks of neutrality, the note said that because the United States had not been a party to, agreed or acquiesced to any of the belligerent countries actions (meaning Britain's 'blockade') and in fact had officially protested as it being against international law it regarded itself '… as free in the present instance to take with a clear conscience and upon accepted principles the position indicated in this note.'

President Wilson's note also suggested that any German Naval commander who presumed an American flag was not being used in good faith and on that presumption alone, destroyed a ship, would be seen as an indefensible violation of neutral rights. It went on to say that if such a situation arose the Imperial Government would be held to 'strict accountability' and steps would be taken to protect American lives and property at sea. The note finished expressing a hope that American vessels will not be molested and accepting the right of Germany to visit and search vessels.

While this note of protest strongly iterates America's attitude to any attack on their merchant ships it is interesting that it concedes the 'rights of visit and search' on the high seas. As always the President seems preoccupied with asserting America's neutrality and the rights that might confer on a non-belligerent. The protest seems almost more passionate in defending the principle than the people and property. This was something that had been protested about to the British Government. Wilson declared at one point that the American people had demanded of him to keep them out of the war but had also demanded that the honour of the United States be upheld at all costs. In early 1916 he warned that both may not be possible.

> … You have bidden me to see that nothing stains or impairs the honour of the United States, and that is a matter not within my control; that depends on what others do, not upon what the Government of the United States does. Therefore there may at any time come a time when I cannot preserve both the honour and the peace of the United States. Do not exact of me an impossible and contradictory thing.[9]

The protest note did not result in the full protection of American life and property. RMS *Lusitania* was not the first sinking by a submarine to result in the loss of American citizens lives and it would not be the last. It was just over seven weeks after Germany's declared date on the exclusion zone (18 February 1915) and five weeks after the protest note of the United States Government, that an American casualty was sustained by a submarine attack. On 27 March 1915 the 4,800-ton *Falaba*, a passenger liner of the Elder Dempster Line, was intercepted and stopped by the German submarine U28. The liner had left Liverpool and was setting out on a voyage to the west coast of Africa. Having stopped the liner, the submarine gave passengers and crew just five minutes to abandon ship and torpedoed it before the evacuation was complete. As a consequence, 104 people were killed. Leon C. Trasher, an American citizen who was a member of the crew, drowned in the incident. A month later an American freighter was attacked by German military force, this time by an aircraft, and while there were no casualties the intent was there and there could have been.[10] On 1 May an American tanker the *Gulflight* was torpedoed without warning off the Scilly Isles and another two American citizens were drowned. These type of incidents were perhaps what President Wilson was referring to when he mentioned the retention of honour later on. Thus there were other vessels which had been sunk by German submarines resulting in the loss of American citizens, although none on the scale of the 121 lost on RMS *Lusitania*.

One of the most often quoted inaccuracies about the sinking of the RMS *Lusitania* was that it brought the United States into the war. This is simply not the case. In pure chronological terms, the RMS *Lusitania* was torpedoed on 7 May 1915. The United States Congress did not approve the declaration of war until 6 April 1917, almost two years after the incident. That is not to say that it didn't contribute to influencing American public opinion, but the fact that America did not enter the war in the immediate wake of the sinking of the RMS *Lusitania* is indicative of the strength of conviction that the American president at the time felt about the status of neutrality. The claim that the sinking was the sole purpose for America's change of heart two years later in many ways undermines the complexity and strategic nature of the neutrality of President Wilson.

Given the dangers that prevailed for American citizens crossing the Atlantic during the war and particularly after the German Declaration in February 1915, there were some US Senators who felt that legislation should be enacted for the prevention of their citizens to take passage on vessels of other nations. Wilson vehemently opposed this. He believed that the rights of citizens of neutral countries had to be protected at all costs. His response to the suggestion of legislation that would inhibit freedom of movement for American citizens across the high seas was unequivocal:

> … No nation, no group of nations, has the right while war is in progress to alter or disregard the principles which all nations have

agreed upon in mitigation of the horrors and sufferings of war; and if the clear rights of American citizens should ever unhappily be abridged or denied by any such action, we should, it seems to me, have in honour no choice as to what our own course should be. For my own part, I cannot consent to any abridgment of the rights of American citizens in any respect. The honour and self-respect of the nation is involved. We covet peace, and shall preserve it at any cost but the loss of honour. To forbid our people to exercise their rights for fear we might have to vindicate them would be a deep humiliation indeed. It would an implicit, all but explicit, acquiescence in the violation of rights of mankind everywhere, and of whatever nation or allegiance …[11]

It was evident then that up to and after the sinking of the RMS *Lusitania* the American stance on its decision to stay out of the war would not be swayed by the loss of some of its citizens. There were protests and they centred on infringement of the rights of neutral citizens but such was Wilson's appreciation of the prospective horror of war that the position of neutrality was to stay in place long after the sinking of RMS *Lusitania*. Many societies, including some of those in the US, clamoured for war. Men, both old and young, often had romantic notions about war, honour and glory. President Wilson it seemed, had a healthy respect of the consequence of war and the tragic impact on any society engaged in it. The sinking of the RMS *Lusitania* was not on its own enough to push the American President into the abyss of global conflict. He did not react immediately and after a period of consideration articulated his views in a speech in which he argued that 'there is such a thing as a man being too proud to fight. There is such a thing as a nation being so right that it does not need to convince others by force that it is right'.[12] Despite this position, he subsequently did send another note of protest on 13 May to the German Government and in this instance it dealt not with the probability of the loss of life but with the reality of it.

It's interesting to note than in the opening paragraphs of the protest note that followed the sinking of the RMS *Lusitania* the President states that he cannot believe that the action had the sanction of the German Imperial Government who had previously had a 'humane and enlightened attitude'. He goes on to acknowledge that the German Government had made a case for the implementation of the 'warzone' in response to Britain's cutting off of Germany's commerce but re-iterates his view that this cannot take away from the rights of American citizens on vessels of any nationality. He acknowledges the requirement that a 'visit and search approach must be taken in checking out the cargo or nationality of a ship that might be a belligerent using a neutral flag to transport contraband'. But in the following paragraph suggests that a submarine cannot effectively carry out this function without disregarding rules of fairness, reason justice and humanity. The note also criticises the warning that appeared in the *New York* newspaper prior to the sailing of the RMS *Lusitania* on two counts: firstly that such a warning purporting to come from the Imperial Government to the citizens of the United States through a newspaper was 'irregular'; secondly that no previous warning of an unlawful act can abate the responsibility for its commission. He then suggests disbelief that the Imperial Government issued specific instructions to attack a ship in this way and that the submarine commanders must have been acting under a misapprehension of orders. President Wilson's note then outlines his expectation that reparations would be made and steps will be taken to prevent anything as subversive to the principles of warfare happening again. The final paragraph is quite forceful:

> The Imperial German Government will not expect the Government of the United States to omit any word or act necessary to the performance of its sacred duty of maintaining the rights of United States and its citizens and of safeguarding their free exercise and enjoyment.[13]

Germany, not surprisingly, responded to the President by telling him firstly that the RMS *Lusitania* had been carrying munitions and secondly that the process of boarding such vessels had been made impossible by Britain's instructions to merchant ships that they had to ram or destroy submarines on sight. Protests against Germany's actions were reported in England, Ireland and elsewhere and much was made of these protests in the British media. In the United States as everywhere else people were horrified by the loss of life that occurred but a large number also vented their anger at Britain. Many letters of protest were sent to newspapers in the US complaining that Britain was being allowed to load dangerous cargo onto passenger ships.

> ... The guilt lies wholly upon the British, who first violated international law by refusing foodstuffs into Germany, and so caused the blockade of the submarines. Also they requested merchantmen to arm themselves, in order to sink submarines or ram them. And now because a submarine saw fit to protect itself by not giving warning and because it prevented ammunition from being landed and used to destroy the lives of their countrymen, all American papers set up a howl. Britain should not use women and children to protect the shipments of contraband ...[14]

Some argued that America's own laws were being flouted and that the ship should never have been allowed to sail from New York. A series of laws and regulations in force from the 1880s and amended several times over the years sought to protect people travelling as passengers to from dangerous cargo. This included military or non-military goods. Quoting section 8 of an 1882 Act, Francis J.A. Dorl, writing in the *Vital Issue* (N.Y.) on 29 May 1915, stated:

> These laws were enacted in 1882 and amended in 1903, 1904 and 1908. Section 8 of the 1882 Act reads as follows: That is shall not be lawful to take, carry or have on board of any such steamship or other vessel any nitro glycerine, dynamite, or any other explosive article or compound, nor any vitriol or like acids, nor gunpowder, except for the ship's use, nor any article or number of articles, whether as cargo or ballast which by reason of the nature or quantity or mode of transport thereof shall either be singly or

collectively, be likely to endanger the health or the lives or the safety of the vessel …[15]

Dorl went on to accuse the Cunard Line of being criminally negligent and suggested the master of the vessel could be jailed under the regulations for up to a year for infringement and the owners of the ship could be open to the charge of manslaughter. Interestingly it had been argued in 1911 by a solicitor of the Department of Commerce that ammunition was cleared to be carried. Other US citizens and some politicians were also exercised by events. Congressman Pearson Hobson wrote to the *New York Times* on 22 May 1915, claiming that a relative of his had been warned not to travel RMS *Lusitania* by a Cunard official. He asked why Cunard had not advised other passengers in the same way. Hobson went on to question many elements of the sinking including why the ship was not advised to take the alternative route around Northern Ireland to avoid the area where submarines were already known to be operating. He questioned the reduction in speed of the RMS *Lusitania*, the absence of a protective convoy and criticised the lack of preparedness for a rescue operation on the south coast of Ireland. He mentioned the Admiralty's instruction to merchant ships and contextualised President Wilson's note of protest in the following paragraph:

> … The order of the British Admiralty instructing British merchantmen to attack and ram German submarines on sight, makes all the British merchant vessels armed and resisting toward German submarines and nullifies their claims in international law to warning and immunity to life from these submarines. Maintaining our position toward Germany, as defined by the President's note, without insisting of the revocation of the British Admiralty's instruction, is equivalent to demanding that German submarines shall not attack British merchant vessels with American lives on board, while these British vessels are free to attack, and are under orders to attack, German submarines.

> So Great Britain could maintain a fleet of merchant vessels
> hunting and destroying German submarines with immunity ...[16]

This view was a criticism of the President's approach in his note to
Germany. As has been shown the note was more about the principle
of an American citizen's inherent right to travel on any ship, even
a belligerent one during the conflict. It ignored the reluctance of
German submarines to either forewarn or board merchant vessels
due to the instruction they were under. American public opinion
varied and there is ample evidence in the letters to newspapers and
other utterances that while there may not be sympathy towards
Germany's position there was certainly lots of criticism of Britain's
strategies of using passenger ships in engagement of the enemy at
sea. Many also criticised the widening of Britain's blockade criteria
that prevented passage of foodstuffs into Germany. President
Wilson later reiterated the points made in the first note in another
communication sent on 9 June and did not address the points made
by Germany in the threat of merchant shipping to the operation of
stop and search strategies.

The President's stand did little to change Germany's tactics;
other vessels were attacked after the RMS *Lusitania* and American
citizens died as a result. But in each case the position of neutrality
was maintained. On 19 August 1915 a British passenger liner of
the White Star Line the *Arabic* was attacked without warning by
a German submarine. The incident occurred when the ship was
westbound from Liverpool and was about 50 miles south of the
Old Head of Kinsale. Forty-four casualties were recorded, including
two American citizens among them. In this instance the American
Government demanded a disavowal of the act and of the submarine
commander over the sinking and Germany conceded it. On 24
March 1916 a ship called the *Sussex* was torpedoed in the English
Channel by a German submarine with the loss of eighty people,
some of whom were American citizens. Wilson had another note
of protest sent to Berlin in which the activities of the German
submarine commanders are suggested to have worsened and become
more frequent. The note again protests against the methodology of

sinking ships using submarines. This objection was not so much about the craft in use by Germany but more about the inability of the submarines and their crews to comply with the cruiser rules which oblige that passengers be taken on board for safety or the ship to be commandeered by German crew. The German Government was accused of continually making promises in respect of not targeting passenger ships and then breaking those promises with continuing disregard for the safety of civilians. The note finishes with a robust warning:

> … the government of the United States is at last forced to the conclusion that there is only one course that it can pursue. Unless the Imperial Government should now immediately declare and effect an abandonment of its present methods of submarine warfare against passenger and freight-carrying vessels, the Government of the United States can have no choice but to sever diplomatic relations with the German Empire altogether. This action the United States contemplates with the greatest reluctance but feels constrained to take in behalf of humanity and the rights of neutral nations.[17]

The German Government responded to the note of protest by agreeing to compel submarine commanders to operate under the cruiser rules. Despite the raising of tensions with Germany there were still problems between Britain and the United States. Britain had increased the restrictions on the capacity of American business to conduct trade. She refused to supply coal or fuel to any ships that were trading with her enemies and unless they signed a pledge to discontinue such trade, they would not be serviced in British ports. They published a 'blacklist' of firms in neutral countries including the US that allied countries were forbidden to deal with.[18]

President Wilson now had difficulties with both sides in the conflict. In December of 1916 he sent a proposal for peace to the government in Berlin and London. He offered himself as an honest broker to assist the governments reaching an agreement to address issues that might end the war. The German Government agreed to meet with their enemies to negotiate peace and the allies also agreed to make whatever sacrifices they needed to in order to uphold their objectives of security and prosperity. The apparent willingness to discuss peace by the German Government was not shared by the German Navy Admirals; they had long argued that an extension of submarine warfare would ensure complete victory and that instead of being restricted by cruiser rules they should be allowed to engage in unrestricted warfare. Others felt that such a strategy would most definitely bring the US into the war on the side of Britain and her allies. The decision was made to undertake unrestricted warfare at the meeting and in a note to the American Government on 31 January the message was conveyed. Wilson broke off diplomatic relations but expressed the view that Germany could be brought round again.

More passenger liners began to be sunk. On 26 February 1917 a British ship *Laconia* was torpedoed and there were twenty-six American citizens among those that died. The same week a telegram from the Foreign Minister Arthur Zimmerman to his counterpart in Washington for onward transmission to Mexico was intercepted by British Intelligence Service. The telegram contained alarming and explosive content for the US:

> We intend to begin on the 1st February unrestricted submarine warfare. We shall endeavour in spite of this to keep the United States of America neutral. In the event of this not succeeding, we make Mexico a proposal of alliance on the following basis: we make war together, make peace together, generous financial support and an understanding on our part that Mexico is to reconquer the lost territory in Texas, New Mexico and Arizona. The settlement in detail is left to you. You will inform the President of the above most secretly as soon as the outbreak of war with the United States is certain and add the suggestion that he should, on his own initiative invite Japan to immediate adherence and at the same time mediate between Japan and ourselves. Please call the President's attention to the fact that the ruthless employment of our submarines now offer the prospect of

compelling England in a few short months to make peace. Signed
Zimmerman.[19]

Other works have cast doubt from time to time over the authenticity
of the telegram, some have even suggested it was concocted by
the British but the telegram and its purported contents had a
significantly bigger impact on American position of neutrality than
the sinking of the RMS *Lusitania*. The direct threat to American
'terra firma' was a far more potent determining factor in the
consideration of German activities that even the submarines. There
was understandably a furore in the United States, in Congress and
on the streets.

When eventually Wilson felt compelled to enter the conflict it
was solely on the basis of the impact on the rights and safety of
American citizens although he did maintain that upholding their
rights also helped uphold the rights of all neutral nations. On
2 April he summoned Congress into special session and addressed
them. He outlined the efforts that had been made to date to protect
the principles of neutrality but concluded that Germany's intentions
represented a war against all nations. Having considered the arming
of merchant vessels to protect American interests he concluded that
such a strategy would soon engulf them in war anyway.

> … With a profound sense of the solemn and even tragical character
> of the step I am taking and of the grave responsibilities which
> it involves but in unhesitating obedience to what I consider my
> constitutional duty, I advise that the Congress declare the recent
> course of the Imperial German government to be in fact nothing
> less than a war against the government and people of the United
> States; that it formally accept the status of belligerent which
> has thus been thrust upon it and that it takes immediate steps
> not only to put the country in a more thorough state of defence
> but also to exert all its power and employ all its resources to
> bring the government of the German Empire to terms and end
> the war …

Many authors have suggested that it was the RMS *Lusitania* that was the heaviest influence on bringing America to war with Germany. However, there were many attempts by the President and his administration to mend fences with Germany and utilise full diplomatic relations and trade with them for the duration of the war after the sinking. In many respects it had nothing to do with RMS *Lusitania*, nothing to do with the arguments proffered by the respective belligerents, nothing to do with the defence of small nations that had been Britain's call to arms after Germany's early incursion into Belgium. America entered the war in April of 1917 against Germany as a result of the direct threat that unrestricted submarine warfare in all oceans represented to the rights of American citizens. The sinking of RMS *Lusitania* had happened a full two years before the US entered the conflict. The incident certainly prompted an articulation of President Wilson's staunchly held beliefs about the rights of American citizens. A right, as he saw it, to travel not just on American ships but even on ships of the belligerents. It also resulted in his portrayal of submarine warfare being totally unacceptable unless governed by the cruiser rules. What the sinking of the RMS *Lusitania* did not do, was bring the United States into the war.

When the US did finally declare their involvement by Congressional agreement on 6 April 1917 they did not have sufficient logistical capacity to get large numbers of troops on the field in Europe immediately. It would be some months before the first units were actively engaged in the land war. However, the US Navy, just eighteen days after America's entry into the war, was sent to the European theatre. Rear Admiral W.S. Sims was appointed to go to London and oversee the co-operative use of American Navy ships and personnel to assist the Royal Navy in the war at sea. He decided that Cobh was to become their base for the duration of the war. Initially a fleet of five US Destroyers under the command of Captain Taussig of the USS *Wadsworth* were deployed. The USS *Conynham*, USS *Porter*, USS *McDougal*, USS *Davis* and USS *Portal* left American shores in April for war in Europe. They arrived in Cobh on 4 May 1917, just a couple of days before the second anniversary

United States victim brought ashore in Cobh (Courtesy *Cork Examiner*)

of the sinking of the RMS *Lusitania*. Admiral Bayly, who had taken over command of the Admiralty at Cobh, sent a number of British Naval vessels out to meet and escort the Americans into port.

The presence of the US Navy had a big impact on Cobh. To facilitate the shore leave of the American sailors, two 'service men' clubs were constructed on the quay beneath Harbour Row. A US Naval Air Station facility was developed at Aghada in the lower Harbour and for the first time in its history, the US Navy brought its own kit-built field hospital and assembled in Whitepoint, Cobh. Previously the Navy had adopted existing buildings for use as hospitals during conflicts but in Cobh they brought the material with them and constructed it on site. The solid house that was in use as the nurses' accommodation block is still there. In addition to the first six ships to arrive many other vessels followed and so in Cobh began a chapter in American and British military co-operation that was truly historic.

11

The Narrative

Understandably, the world was shocked at the news of the loss of so much life on the RMS *Lusitania*. Newspapers grappled to provide their readers with the very latest news. Speculation was rife, outrage was widespread. Initial reports were sometimes inaccurate claiming two, three or more torpedoes were fired at the ship. Harrowing scenes of the destruction of the ship and the loss of life by drowning were outlined with few questioning the sinister presence of munitions on board that undoubtedly added to the magnitude of the tragedy. Every one of the 1,198 passengers that died that day had family or friends, loved ones or parents, children or grandchildren. Apart from the immediate bereavement of these closest of relatives, people who knew nobody were outraged at the manner in which people had died. Mostly, the passengers were ordinary people going about routine tasks of travel, holiday or business. They had no argument with the people of Germany or the Kaiser. Even if the British people's government was at war with Germany, they themselves were non-combatants. The 140 citizens of the United States that were on board were even further removed from motivation to attack them as their government had stayed deliberately neutral since the conflict had begun.

Few of the passengers would have had an intimate knowledge of seafaring, of lifeboat deployment or sea survival techniques. Surely then it behoved the Cunard shipping company and the Admiralty to have given them fair warning. Warning about the contents of the ship, the exclusion zone that had been imposed which they would pass through on their intended voyage. And finally warnings about the deadly activities of the German fleet of submarines that were by that time sinking civilian ships at will in these areas. But a particular narrative had already been created even before the RMS *Lusitania* was torpedoed. Survivors interviewed after the event said they had believed that the RMS *Lusitania* could outrun any submarine and that it was fast enough to do so. This is the fastest ship on the ocean they were told, nothing can catch it. The speed of the RMS *Lusitania* was indeed much faster than that of a submarine; however, the argument does not apply if the ship is sailing towards the submarine.

Many passengers who boarded the RMS *Lusitania* that day were under the illusion that their lives were not in danger. The Cunard shipping company, it appears, did little to make them any wiser. The combination of the ship actually being attacked and the great human loss of life created fertile ground into which a lasting narrative could be sown.

Like all wars the acquisition and collection of information about enemy intentions, practices and movements in the First World War became a crucial element of strategic planning. There were numerous intelligence agencies and branches of the armed forces tasked with the gathering of information on an array of fronts. The Admiralty's intelligence arm was located in Whitehall, London. Any information emanating from Germany or relating to Germany and its allies could be of use in conflict. Wireless transmissions, letters, verbal information or written publications were intercepted where possible and collected for interpretation and future use. From the beginning of the war, both sides used coded messaging for transmission to troops, ships, planes and submarines. In August of 1914 a German warship ran aground off the coast of Estonia and the Russians salvaged the explanatory codebooks in use by Germany at the time. In September these were given to the British. In London, a group of experts were formed to intercept and explain the meaning of transmissions in great secrecy in a room in the Admiralty building numbered 40.

In this way the expression 'Room 40', became associated with the epicentre of British Admiralty counterintelligence. After the codebooks had been received, Admiralty codebreakers there were in a position to provide the most comprehensive details of German submarine activities and movements. They could know the time and day of departure and the intended route and targets of specific submarines. They had information regarding naval stores for the fleet, crew numbers and movements, maintenance periods, repairs, losses and successes. Questions still remain about the dissemination of information by this branch and the time-lag between receiving the information and advising shipping about it. There were often periods of twenty-four hours or more when the Admiralty at Cobh were being advised of movements and hostile actions of submarines off the coast of Ireland. Warning and incidents that had occurred a day earlier were of little use to those at sea. In response to criticisms about not sending detailed information to ships like RMS *Lusitania*, it was usually argued that such practices would alert the German intelligence agencies to the fact that their code had been broken. Such a development would result in the loss of a great tactical advantage. Thus, most communications were vague and generalised.

The Germans had stated very publicly in February of 1915 that they were imposing exclusion zones around the British Isles in response to the Royal Navy's ever-tightening blockade around the North Sea, a blockade that was inhibiting legitimate civilian trade. The narrative of the day rarely casts the submarine campaign against civilian ships in this context. Instead they were depicted as marauding harbingers of doom. For those who suffered from submarines attacks this is a perhaps a fitting description; however, the strategic intention of Germany was the same as that of Britain: to have a stranglehold over the trade and economic lifelines of their enemy. It is interesting to note that unlike the British blockade which targeted and impeded ships of all countries, the German 'blockade' was initially targeted only at Britain's ships and her allies and vessels in the designated zone. There was a point at which Germany was only going to prevent enemy ships access. They promised safe passage to ships of neutral countries and encouraged citizens of neutral countries to travel only on shipping companies of neutral countries.

For those travelling on the RMS *Lusitania* prior warning had been given that any person travelling on an enemy ship was standing themselves into danger.

NOTICE!

Passengers intending to embark on the Atlantic voyage are reminded that a state of war exists between Germany and her allies and Great Britain and her allies; that the zone of war includes the waters adjacent to the British Isles; that in accordance with formal notice given by the Imperial German Government, vessels flying the flag of Great Britain or of any of her allies, are liable to destruction in those waters and that travellers sailing in the war zone on ships of Great Britain and her allies, do so at their own risk.

Imperial German Embassy, 22 April 1915[1]

The narrative created in the wake of the sinking was that the warning that appeared in the newspaper the day before RMS *Lusitania* sailed was a direct threat to the ship. However, it was a general warning to all shipping of neutral countries and did not mention RMS *Lusitania* at all. In fact the notice was dated at least a week before. But in the newspaper the warning was positioned in such a way as to be beside the advertisement for the RMS *Lusitania* trans-Atlantic service and so it was construed as being a direct threat. The notice, however, clearly directs its message at travellers who may decide to travel on any ship with a British Flag or any ship under the flag of Britain's allies. Nowhere does it mention the RMS *Lusitania*. Yet the narrative that evolved or was created around the notice was that it was a threat to the RMS *Lusitania* and an indication of premeditative action to deliberately attack a ship in order to kill civilians.

However, a number of points should be noted. Britain was using civilian ships to carry munitions across the Atlantic Ocean. Britain was formally at war with Germany and her allies so those weapons and munitions were for intended use against Germany. Britain was instructing her civilian ships to ram submarines on sight. Britain was deploying civilian ships as decoys to attract German submarines into the line of fire of British submarines. Britain was arming civilian vessels with the intention of attacking German submarines. In both the passenger and the decoy vessels, the flags of many countries were being used. Britain's Navy was causing the interruption of supplies of foodstuffs and food manufacturing equipment into Germany directly impacting on its civilian non-combatant population. Germany gave forewarning to the world of its intention to extend the warzone around Ireland and Britain. Germany outlined its intention to attack and destroy ships sailing under the British flag or that of her allies anywhere they found them. Germany offered unimpeded passage to ships of neutral countries through the warzone. It seems that none of these issues, some of which had a direct bearing on the sort of action that led to the sinking of the RMS *Lusitania*, were included in the general narrative at the time. To this day some people consider the RMS *Lusitania* as the first in attack against civilians, some believe it happened out of the blue with no warning whatsoever and, more importantly, some still believe that the attack was totally unjustified.

Many later believed that the United States entered the war immediately and that the RMS *Lusitania* was the incident that triggered an instant response. As has been shown earlier, this was clearly not the case. That these beliefs still persist today is a testament to the work done in shaping a particular view for the public at large. A horrified public sought explanations for such a despicable loss of life. They were eager to contextualise what had happened and gain an understanding as to how it had come to this. Unaware for the most part of the intrigue and shadowy world of intelligence, subterfuge and political posturing, they were hungry to grasp any explanation for the sinking. The vacuum in understanding the complexity of the incident was filled by creating a vision of German maliciousness and brutishness. Accusations of pre-meditated intent abounded. In Kinsale, the day after the sinking, a coroner's inquest on the bodies of a number of victims who had been washed ashore concluded that this was a 'murderous act' perpetrated by the Kaiser, the German Navy and the German people.

Various unfounded claims were made regarding the number of torpedoes that struck the ship. It was also suggested at one point that there were several submarines that had lain in wait for the RMS *Lusitania* before attacking it in concert with each other. Despite the fact that most survivors attested to a second explosion occurring after the torpedo struck, the public debate appeared to have been steered away successfully from questioning the origin of this explosion. Official enquiries did little to shed light on the reason for the second massive explosion that seemed to have been the one that doomed the liner to sink in such a speedy fashion. The board of trade investigation into the sinking also became a tool in the shaping of the narrative that was to persist over the years. Lord Mersey was asked to chair a court of investigation. However, he was given a fixed set of questions which had to be answered or investigated and his remit did not go beyond them. There were no questions asked about the amount of information provided to passengers about the nature of some of the cargo. There were no questions asked about what exact cargo was carried for and by the Admiralty. There were no questions asked about whether or not the British Admiralty intelligence regarding the movement of submarines on the south coast that day. There were no questions asked about the nature of the second explosion. There were no questions asked about the general use of civilian ships by Great Britain and whether or not such a practice would contribute to the vulnerability of passenger ships. There were no questions asked about the actions of HMS *Juno* and where she might have received her instruction from. Instead a narrow, presumptive conclusion was arrived at which did not consider any culpability or blame on the part of Cunard, the Admiralty of the British Government.

MERSEY REPORT:
The Court, having carefully enquired into the circumstances of the above-mentioned disaster, finds, for the reasons appearing in

the annex hereto, that the loss of the said ship and lives was due to damage caused to the said ship by torpedoes fired by a submarine of German nationality whereby the ship sank. In the opinion of the Court the act was done not merely with the intention of sinking the ship, but also with the intention of destroying the lives of the people on board.

It was the German submarine and its captain that fired the torpedo. It was their actions alone that caused the physical sinking of the ship and the death of so many.

However, the magnitude of the disaster, the sheer number of people who were lost, was clearly increased by the content of whatever it was that ignited after the first explosion caused by the torpedo. And perhaps also increased by the recalling of the HMS *Juno* from close to the scene of the disaster and thereby being made unavailable to rescue people from drowning. Undoubtedly, the popular narrative perpetrated at the time that the RMS *Lusitania* could easily outrun any submarine threat also contributed to passengers having insufficient information to make a well-informed decision about their safety and whether or not to travel. The Mersey inquiry did not ask any questions about who had been responsible for these matters and so a narrative blossomed over the years that cast the German's sinking of the ship as an isolated barbaric action with no mitigating circumstances.

While the narrative has been challenged by many writers and scholars over the years there has probably been an over emphasis on the nature of the cargo that caused the second explosion. Thousands of words have been written speculating on what it was that exploded. Although it remains an important question, its relevance has diminished; whether it was explosive powder used in the assembly of shells, whether it was the filled cases of shrapnel, whether it was an industrial type explosion of aluminium or the presence of gun cotton does not take from the fact that the ship was carrying munitions and in that context was a perfectly legitimate target in time of war. One fact that remains undisputed but does not find its way into the narrative is that the Cunard shipping company endangered human life by using their 'passenger' ship to transport munitions. Even in modern conflicts the world at large has been quick to label such actions as the use of innocent civilians as 'human shields'. This question, together with the very legitimate question regarding the actions of HMS *Juno* and the consequence of utilising the services of civilian ships during the war, needs to be brought centre stage in order to broaden the very narrow consideration of this incident.

The German submarine fired the torpedo and in doing so almost guaranteed that the ship would be damaged and possibly sunk with loss of life. They must bear responsibility for that and blame was apportioned to them and rightly so. The Germans, on witnessing the rapid sinking of the ship, could have stayed and recovered some people from the water. It had been done before. But they didn't, thereby adding to the numbers that perished. They must bear responsibility for that too. But they were not responsible for the cargo that the ship carried. And it was the cargo that made her a legitimate target. Cunard must bear responsibility for the carriage of military cargo. The crew of HMS *Juno* operated a ship that was deployed to assist merchant ships and make the warzone safer for the passage of Britain's merchant ships through it. They were not responsible for the German submarine attacking vessels but they were a ship that could be used for the rescue effort. That they were called back when on their way to the RMS *Lusitania* certainly added to the number of people that drowned. Those who ordered the ship to turn around and return to Cobh bear that responsibility. These are issues that have not found their way into the general population's understanding of the events.

Instead of people generally thinking it was a 'savage attack on an innocent vessel that brought America into the war' can the narrative not be widened to include a 'deadly attack on a vessel carrying munitions with the loss of life inordinately increased by its cargo and the failure of some ships to render aid to those that were cast into the sea'? America's neutrality had nothing to do with the sinking of RMS *Lusitania*. The position of the United States had no relevance to the sinking so why has it remained such a popular social myth that it brought the US into the war? Certainly, Wilson's continued protestations about the use of the submarine may merit a connection from the RMS *Lusitania* to the eventual entry of the US into the conflict but it is only a tenuous connection. Between 7 May 1915 and the opening months of 1917, the United States still engaged with Germany as a legitimate foreign sovereignty who had a right to at least stop and inspect ships. Wilson also implied the right of Germany to destroy ships thought to be carrying munitions once passengers were first brought to safety. His biggest problem with the use of submarines was not about their capacity to unleash lethal power against general shipping but their incapacity to carry innocent passengers and comply with a version of the cruiser rules. His insistence that all US and other neutral citizens should be shielded from any dangers when travelling on belligerent ships, even those carrying munitions, positioned aspirations above practicalities. If followed, Britain or any enemy of Germany would have been free to import any manner of explosives, munitions or ammunition on any vessel and with the inclusion of a single neutral passenger would enjoy immunity from attack. Such a request could never have been conceded in the crucial business of supply of military equipment and materials in time of war. Despite the impossibility of Germany to deliver on Wilson's impractical requests, that they discontinue using submarines for contraband interception, he continued to engage with the German Government long after the sinking of RMS *Lusitania*.

12

The Wreck

The wreck of the RMS *Lusitania* still lies in a relatively shallow watery grave just off the coast of Cork. From the 1980s to the time of writing the wreck is owned by an American entrepreneur, F. Gregg Bemis Jr. He bought it from the London Liverpool War Reclamations Board. There have been numerous legal challenges to his ownership and title. Among them the British Admiralty court in 1985, the Federal District Court in America in 1994 and the High Court in Ireland in 1996. None of the challenges were successful and he still is the legal owner of the ship. His stated objectives for the RMS *Lusitania* are to continue to attempt to reveal her secrets 'and the creation of museum exhibits and educational displays to stimulate interest in the important place she holds in international history ...' [1] Mr Bemis believes that the ultimate conclusive evidence surrounding the wreck will only be gained when a thorough exploration of the entire wreck takes place.

RMS *Lusitania* is resting at a depth of 295ft beneath the surface. Despite its relatively shallow location, the visibility is constantly poor there. Earlier attempts to dive on the wreck were hampered by the lack of light and the swirling underwater currents that make it a very hostile location in which to conduct any research. The ship came to rest on its starboard side which was the side that was struck by the U20's torpedo. It has been dived on many times yet there are still numerous secrets that the hulk holds within. Dr Robert Ballard, who had discovered the location of *Titanic* and dived on both it and the *Bismarck*, became interested in the RMS *Lusitania*. He embarked on an exploratory expedition to the ship in 1993. Unlike the previously mentioned vessels he did not have to search for the location of the ship as its position was well known. He used advanced technology of the day to create high-resolution images that provide a very clear picture of the condition and position of the ship as she lay at that time. In addition he assembled a team of experts, among them the great maritime artist, Ken Marschall. His artistic expertise was to provide images of the findings and also representations of what the ship looked like that were far superior to the limited black and white photographic pictures that people had become accustomed to when researching elements of the ships history. Dr Ballard had at his disposal, a mini submarine named *Delta*, a remotely operated vehicle, *Jason*, and two small robotic vehicles called *Medea* and *Homer*. All were operated, controlled or directed from the command vessel, *Northern Horizon*, which was on station directly above the wreck. After initial sonar mapping the robotic vehicles were deployed and began to send back television type images to the command vessel. Ballard describes the images thus: 'The legend has been humbled. She lies broken and battered, most of her superstructure gone, many of her portside doors thrown wide open, a sorry shadow of her former self.'[2]

Ballard was not the first to explore the RMS *Lusitania*. The Admiralty were there many years before him. John Light, who at one time was a business partner of Gregg Bemis, dived on the wreck on about forty occasions. He only spent a few minutes each time. Later advances in mixed-gas diving afforded longer times on site. Chris Reynolds, an Irish Navy diver, was one of the first so called 'technical' divers to descend to the wreck on mixed gas in 1994. At the time there had been an Irish diver called Des Quiggley who was attempting to gather an Irish diving team to be the first to visit the wreck using new 'technical' methods of mixed gas. However, an American team led by Polly Tapson got there ahead of him. She and her partner John Chapman invited Lieutenant Reynolds to accompany them on their dive. During his career in the navy he had headed up the Naval Diving section on Haulbowline. He wrote an account of the dive for the military publication *An Cosantoir* and recalls descending to the wreck. At the time of writing in 2014 he still has a vivid recollection of his first visit to the depths.

I landed on the bow of the ship and visibility was zero with the naked eye. When our lamps were switched on however the water was crystal clear. She was a beautiful ship with magnificent fittings. I clearly remember running my hands along the name 'RMS Lusitania' along her bow and can still feel the name under my fingers. We only had twenty minutes on the wreck and had to include a two and a half hour period for ascent to the surface. During the time there we were able to get into the lamp lockers near the base of the forward mast. These contained the emergency lamps in case there was a failure of the navigation lights they could be mounted on the superstructure of the ship. They were almost six feet tall and were crafted to the highest standards. Almost a work of art. The ports and windows were visible and the rectangular ports for the first class accommodation had intricate filigree like designs on them.[3]

Reynolds also noted at the time of his first dive how hazardous the wreck of RMS *Lusitania* had become. He described the ship being covered in layers of fishing nets snagged on the superstructure and waving gently in the currents that swirled around the ship. In his estimation it was a most dangerous place to dive and the highest standards and expertise were required to avoid fatalities down there. During his second dive he was accompanied by a civilian who got into difficulty and had to be evacuated to a decompression chamber on the Naval Base.

Controversy later surrounded the incident and legal proceedings followed. It was during this time that a fellow diver announced that she had spotted a tube on the wreck containing the paintings of Hugh Lane. Reynolds claims this was a complete fabrication designed to divert attention away from the negative publicly that was focussed previously on the competence of the dive team.

It was only in 2011, on an exploratory expedition to the wreck led by owner Mr Bemis, that the images of .303 rifle munitions on board were broadcast globally for the first time. Irish diver Eoin McGarry had recovered several rounds earlier in 2008. On this occasion he was the dive supervisor for a National Geographic television documentary. They managed to get a camera into one of the holds and the munitions could be seen in colour on television screens around the world. If there was any doubt about the presence of munitions before, there is certainly none now. What was noteworthy about the images of the munitions was that they were unexploded. So researchers are still left with the questions surrounding the second explosion.

The same documentary that revealed the presence of the rounds of ammunition also tried to seek an explanation for the second explosion. They explored the frequently quoted explanations such as exploding boilers, spontaneous combustion of coal dust and the presence of highly explosive powder used in artillery shells. The documentary sought the assistance of a scientific facility in the United States that simulates and studies the nature of explosions. Scientists there were able to recreate the exact conditions that would equate to the spontaneous combustion of coal dust. They found from their research that there would have been insufficient energy produced by the combustion of the coal dust to cause the destructive power which sank the ship. The same methodology of testing also discounted the theory of exploding boilers as a cause of the massive damage that resulted in the foundering of the RMS *Lusitania*. Another suggestion had been that a consignment of aluminium powder, of a type that was used in the composition of certain artillery shells, ignited after the torpedo impacted. The television documentary also discounted this theory. They reported that there would have been enough explosive power in dust cloud of aluminium. However, they explained that such a combustion and subsequent explosion would always be accompanied by a very white blinding light. They cited that there were no reports from any of the eyewitness about the occurrence of such a white blinding light and so it couldn't have been the aluminium. Paddy O'Sullivan, in his decades of extensive research on the mystery of the second explosion has a different view. He points out that aluminium dust can become highly explosive under a wide range of conditions. In fact, he spent many years carrying out 'home experiments' on spoonfuls of aluminium dust with repeated results of a high degree of explosive consequences to the ignition of the dust. He believes this is what caused the second explosion and concludes, '… the second explosion that rocked the RMS *Lusitania* was nothing more sinister than an industrial accident'.[4] The National Geographic dismissal of the aluminium dust explosion may have been a little hasty. If a mid-air explosion occurred from an artillery shell during its airborne trajectory a white blinding light would certainly be expected. In the case of the RMS *Lusitania*, the explosion occurred beneath the waterline. Before the effect of the explosion reaches daylight it will have travelled through pipework containing a variety of liquids – waste water from sinks, showers, baths and scuppers, tanks or receptacles containing grease, oil, fuel – or any number of materials that could affect the 'colour' of an explosion. Even if the aluminium-induced explosion had been a blinding white light to begin with, would it remain so after ripping through pipework, tanks and materials that was in close proximity at the time of impact? With the proof from the scientific facility in the US that featured in the National Geographic documentary that the explosive impact of the aluminium was enough to sink the ship, with Paddy O'Sullivan's own research-based beliefs and with consideration of the impact of proximate materials impacting on the resultant colour of the explosive plume, it seemed probable that the second explosion was caused as suggested by the consignment of aluminium.

Suggestions about the bottom of the ship being completely 'blown out' have been impossible to confirm because of the way the ship is lying on its side. Also it can be taken with some semblance of certainty that the shrapnel shells didn't explode either. None of the visits to the wreck have ever reported the pepper holes that would result in such shrapnel piercing the hull of the ship. If they exploded surely there would have been some sign of the effects on the surrounding steelwork off the ship itself.

Eoin McGarry is an Irish diver who has spent more time on the wreck of the RMS *Lusitania* than anybody else in all the time since she has been on the ocean floor. This soft-spoken rather modest man knows the wreck of the RMS *Lusitania* intimately. McGarry made his first dive to the RMS *Lusitania* wreck in 2005 and has dived the wreck four sometimes five times every year since. He's proud of the fact that he has spent more time on the wreck than anyone else and explains that despite the number of dives undertaken by John Light, he was only at the sight for about five minutes each time. Eoin, on the other hand, spends twenty-five to thirty minutes on the numerous dives per year that he makes. He recalls his first dive to the RMS *Lusitania* clearly:

> When I descended I arrived at the bow of the ship. I was struck by the sheer size of the wreck and the robust fittings and fixtures still visible. The physical presence of the huge liner then raises the notion of the fact that so many people died on her. It is an awesome and eerie experience. The personal items that are visible around the debris field tell their own tragic story too. A coroner told me that when a body sinks to a depth of more than forty metres the usual release of gases which raise bodies to the surface are counter balanced by the water column preventing them from floating upwards. What this meant to me was that wherever I saw a pair of shoes or a personal item in the sand on the bottom, an actual person had lain there. It was a powerful reminder of the human tragedy that occurred when the ship sank. Today the ships is a tangled mess.[5]

McGarry has recovered numerous items from the RMS *Lusitania*, all brought up in accordance with the protective legislation that governs wreck and historical sites. He has filmed and photographed the entire ship and entered any spaces that were possible. But he believes there were numerous illegal dives on the wreck where there was no regard for the integrity of the ship and its history.

Prior to 1994 all that was needed to dive on the wreck was the owner's permission. In 1995 in a sensational claim about the presence of Hugh Lane paintings on the ship the Irish government imposed a 'Heritage Order' that had the effect of containing access to the wreck and imposing strict regulations for the removal of any items from the wreck itself. In essence you have to have the permission of the owner to salvage anything and then you have to comply with multiple regulations that govern these matters.

While such regulations are designed to protect the integrity of the ship, it would appear that the designation of the site as having not just historical and cultural value, but archaeological value too creates major problems for divers like McGarry. Before any item can be recovered from the site reams of forms have to be filled out in seeking specific permissions, methodologies and licencing. There then has to be an impact assessment on the surrounding area and the job becomes heavily burdened by bureaucratic considerations rather than what it is practical or possible to retrieve. Both he and the owner disagree with its designation as an archaeological site. They agree it is historical and cultural but not archaeological. There is an important distinction here because the label archaeological confers a much stricter regime than the other two. There are numerous definitions of archaeology in different dictionaries:

Archaeology: the study of human history and prehistory through the excavation of sites and the analysis of artefacts and other physical remains. (Oxford)
Archaeology: the excavation and subsequent study of the physical remains of earlier civilizations, especially buildings and artefacts, which now benefits from advances in scientific techniques such as carbon dating. (Chambers 21st Century)
Archaeology: the study of man's past by scientific analysis of the material remains of his cultures. (Collins)
Archaeology: the study of the buildings, graves, tools, and other objects that belonged to people who lived in the past, in order to learn about their culture and society. (Cambridge)

Archaeology: the study of ancient societies, done by looking at tools, bones, buildings, and other things from that time that have been found. (Bing)

Other than the Cambridge entry it would appear that the general idea is that archaeology is the study of artefacts, buildings and sites in order for us to learn about ancient societies or people about whom we know little or have no other means of learning. Even in the Cambridge definition it refers to archaeology as a means to learn about culture and society. Both Bemis and McGarry argue that the RMS *Lusitania* is not an archaeological site in the definitions of the word precisely because we already know so much about the people on board the ship, the ship itself and indeed the society of the time. There are many independent sources that can teach us about this era. McGarry believes that having the RMS *Lusitania* subjected to the same confines of an archaeological site makes it so difficult that it will drive legitimate divers away from conducting dives there. This he fears will lead to illegal rogue dives returning where there will be no regard whatsoever for the integrity and historical importance of the ship. He laughs at the denials that the Royal Navy ever depth charged the wreck of the RMS *Lusitania* as he has photographs of actual unexploded 'Hedgehog' depth charges that were carried on British Corvettes.

Despite these difficulties, McGarry has retrieved some artefacts from the wreck. Among them is one of the two wheelhouse telemotors which was operated by the ship's wheel (helm) and used to control the steering of the rudder on the ship. A 'Turbine Tell Indicator' indicator which was mounted on the deck head (ceiling) of the bridge to indicate the current state of engines (like a modern day rev counter) and what level of propulsion they were delivering ahead or astern. A sidelight (porthole) and a port window from the superstructure. These were all brought to the surface under the Irish Government issued licence number 07-D-010 from the dive in 2011. Other than the porthole, which was gifted to him by Bemis, all other artefacts are destined for a new museum that is to be built in

Salvaged window port from RMS *Lusitania*. (© Michael Martin)

Turbine tell indicator from RMS *Lusitania*. (© Michael Martin)

Kinsale County Cork, near the Old Head of Kinsale and in sight of the area where the RMS *Lusitania* met her fate.

When McGarry was asked about the view of some people who believe that taking artefacts from a wreck constitutes plundering a gravesite he rejects such a notion and underlines his view that this is historical research of the most ethical kind. He relates how during the many lectures he presented around the country relatives of those who were lost on the ship are pleased and emotionally moved by the simple act of touching something that belonged to the ship. He believes they derive comfort and connections from this. 'It provides focus for them in recalling their family history loved ones.' Having met with McGarry in the pleasant surroundings of his County

Waterford home it is evident that he has a highly developed respect for the wreck and the people who died on the ship. The enormity of the human tragedy is palpable when touching these artefact's and now, thanks to enthusiasts like McGarry, people will be able to see them for themselves when they are installed with all due regard for their important heritage into a public museum.

McGarry on his many dives to the wreck has seen munitions and materials used in the construction of weapons and shells. There is ample evidence of them. He is not convinced that the second explosion was caused by aluminium, as suggested by Paddy O'Sullivan, arguing that the milling process during that period of particle size of the aluminium was too big to be suspended in the air

Eoin McGarry and a port from RMS *Lusitania*. (© Michael Martin)

for long enough to create the fine dust cloud formation that would be required for it to become explosive by a secondary ignition source. However, O'Sullivan points to explosions that occurred in milling factories in the US at that time.

Whatever the actual cause of the second explosion, the present-day RMS *Lusitania* is a sad reflection of her former glory. Footage from the cameras of Eoin McGarry and others reveal a tangle of twisted and broken materials and fittings in a dangerous and hostile environment.

The U20 was also to end up as a wreck. Under the command Kapitanleutnant Schwieger the submarine went to the aid of another off the coast of Denmark and ran aground. Efforts to release her failed and the captain decided to blow her up rather than let it fall into enemy hands. There would have been a natural fear that a vessel like a submarine if it fell into enemy hands would become a great source of counter intelligence. Already in the war crucial information had been gathered from a vessel captured by a Russian submarine. Numerous parts of the wreck were taken and are on display in various museums in Denmark and elsewhere.[6] Schwieger was decorated for gallantry in July of 1917 by the German Government for his prolific record in sinking 190,000 tons of merchant shipping. He died in September 1917 during the war at the age of 32, being lost with all of his crew on the U88 when they struck a submerged mine. Ironically, the fatal encounter was as a result of being pursued by a Q ship, HMS *Stonecrop*.[7]

Conclusion

There is no doubt that the sinking of the RMS *Lusitania* was a human tragedy of great proportions. There is no justification for the slaughter of innocent non-combatants. The terror of an explosion at sea resulting in the injury, disfigurement and death of human beings is no different in many respects from the terror rained upon civilian populations in land-based communities in war-torn regions where international conflict is played out. It should never be enough just to decry the act itself as unacceptable. Such tragedies deserve a more detailed examination of the events than just criticising the perpetrators. As in all acts, there are circumstance, perspectives, consequences and, hopefully, explanations.

In the case of RMS *Lusitania*, as in many tragedies, the perpetrators were not the only participants. The shipping company, the citizen's respective governments and the ship's captain all have varying roles to play with varying degrees of responsibility. It appears that little responsibility was ever attached to most of the above mentioned other than the German Navy. The narrative that was created at the time – this was an action that plumbed new depths of inhumanity for which the German's were solely responsible – fitted comfortably into the British propaganda narrative, allowing them to portray the Germans as a savage, immoral enemy. The reality in the First World War was that innocent civilians in their hundreds of thousands were killed during the conflict by all participants and later carpet bombing of cities by both sides during the Second World War was done in the knowledge that countless innocent civilians would be killed. Numerically these particular killings were far in excess of those killed on RMS *Lusitania*. None of this detracts from the injustice of non-combatants being killed in war, but to present the sinking of the RMS *Lusitania* as some sort of milestone in a league of barbarity is to ignore the loss of millions of lives in other conflicts throughout the ages.

It also ignores the responsibility that other participants in the tragedy. At what point does the responsibility of the Cunard shipping company towards its fare paying passengers begin and end? They accepted payment from civilians for a journey across the Atlantic into a known 'danger zone' that had been notified in writing to all prospective shipping companies and travellers. The German High Command felt the necessity to issue a warning in a New York newspaper on the day the ship sailed, advising prospective passengers about the existence of the exclusion zone and the inherent threat that travelling through it posed. The advert was presented in the subsequent narrative as being an indication of Germany's evil intentions towards RMS *Lusitania* but was it not a responsible measure advising people of real danger?

It would appear that the advice and threats of the German Navy were dismissed on the basis that the speed of RMS *Lusitania* was so much greater than that of any submarines in service at that time. Hoehling & Hoehling attribute numerous such comments to Captain Turner from eyewitness and, in a conversation with the press in the company of Vanderbilt and Frohman, he is reputed to have said:

> do you think all these people would be booking on the RMS *Lusitania* if they thought she could be caught by a German submarine? Why it's the best joke I've heard in many days, this talk of torpedoing. Germany can concentrate her entire fleet of submarines in our track and we would elude them.[1]

The ship itself could comfortably travel two or three times as fast as any submarine which is significant if the submarine is behind you – but not if it were lurking, unseen, in front. Were the reassurances given that the speed of the ship itself was enough to reduce the possibility of attack sufficient or even valid? There are quite a number of circumstances in which the ability to outrun a submarine would be beneficial and would result in escape. However, if the planned course of a voyage is running towards and through a noted zone where there is a certainty that danger awaits one must question the wisdom of embarking on such a voyage.

There were laws place in the USA for the protection of people sailing on passengers ships. These laws were flouted by the operators and owners of the RMS *Lusitania* when they allowed the ship to carry munitions. A very generous interpretation might be able to establish that there was no breach of the 'law' in the carrying of .303 Remington bullets, as they might not have been considered a danger to passengers in their own right, but these were being transported for the war effort and their presence on the ship certainly was a danger to passengers, in that they positioned the ship as one that was carrying war making materials for use against the enemy and thus making it a legitimate target.

In today's parlance, this raises a question over the Cunard line's 'duty of care' towards its passengers and staff. Again from today's perspective, is there an arguement that the people on board that ship from New York on 1 May 1915 were effectively being used as human shields?

It is safe to assume that not a single passenger would have embarked on that journey if they knew in advance that they would be killed. How many would have gone if they had been told that of the 1,257 passengers on the ship they would have 62 per cent chance of <u>not</u> surviving the journey? Of course nobody knew that anybody would die, least of all Cunard. But did they not fully consider the risks that were confronting them? Should the passengers have been told that this ship was carrying munitions and consequently that the ship could be deemed to be a legitimate target?

RMS *Lusitania* was not an innocent ship. She was acting under instructions from the Admiralty in Great Britain. She was carrying munitions and explosive materials that endangered and subsequently killed some of her passengers. She was in breach of the spirit of American Law that had been designed to protect the travelling public. She knowingly took on those materials, despite the presence of innocent passengers on board. It doesn't matter if it was explosive powder for use in weapons or an industrial product, the result was the same.

The twenty-one questions that were posed by the Board of Trade Enquiry into the tragedy chaired by Lord Mersey were very narrow in what they sought to establish. They were geared towards establishing the cause of the physical loss of the ship and whether or not the ship and its owners complied with the technical observance of the law. They did not include many of those questions that are outlined above. They certainly did not look at preventive measures that might have been carried out by Cunard.

Another question arises about the responses, instructions and actions of the Admiralty and the Royal Navy. Much was made of their instructions to Turner and other captains about how best to deter the attack of submarines. Ships masters were advised to undertake certain measures when they reached the 'danger zone'. They were advised, among other things, to swing out the lifeboats to prepare for swift evacuation of passengers should an attack occur. All watertight doors were to be closed. There was a recommendation to double the lookouts to increase the possibility of early detection of any periscopes and conning towers; another to stay away from headlands and port entrances where submarines reputedly lurked in waiting. They were told to stay mid-channel on entering the Irish Sea. Finally ships masters were advised when in the exclusion zone to adopt a zigzag course that would deviate from the usual single heading course coming from mid-Atlantic. All of these measures were to be applied on reaching the 'danger zone' around Great Britain and Ireland. The advices on lifeboats and lookouts appear to make good sense; however, there are questions that must be raised about the value of adopting a zigzag pattern of passage through the 'danger zone'.

The idea advanced by the Admiralty was that if a zigzag pattern was adopted by a merchant ship, this would somehow decrease the possibility of being intercepted. There were even different patterns of zigzagging suggested to ships' masters by the Admiralty.[2] Some stayed on one leg of a course for a different length of time to another leg. Some changed course more often and at irregular intervals. One can accept that a break in the pattern of course and speed lessens the chance of predicting a particular passage. But the fact that there were crafted patterns in itself inferred a certain predictability. It was thought that a submarine or other surface craft would, in certain situations, be forced to mount an attack in a shorter time frame if they knew the course of their intended target ship might change at any moment.

However, zigzagging is only relevant to the ship's course; it is merely a temporary deviation from the usual straight line of a ship's intended heading and a zigzag course is longer than a straight one, meaning that it takes more time to get from A to B. If the submarine is unaware of a ship's presence the way in which the ship manoeuvres has no relevance to anything other than the fact that zigzagging will keep the ship in a particular area for longer than was necessary to complete the voyage. If a submarine sights a ship of superior speed which is out of range of its weapons, it is actually aided by the delay that zigzagging would cause. If the ships course, on the other hand, happens to be coming towards the submarine, it is then the case that the ship will actually come from a position where it is 'out of range' as a target to coming 'into range' as a potential target. Again a zigzag pattern in that circumstance gives the submarine more time to prepare to mount the attack.

Captain Turner was criticised for not adopting this type of course when he entered the danger zone; some argued that by not zigzagging he stood his ship into danger. However, it seems evident that the zigzagging pattern insisted upon by the Admiralty was more often an advantage to the submarine than the merchant ship. It can be argued that the unpredictability of a course was an advantage and mounted a challenge for those submarines trying to 'line up a shot'. However, the proficiency of submarines crews meant that the preparation and loading of a torpedo could be done very quickly from the time that a potential target was spotted. Added to which, in the case of the RMS *Lusitania*, a change in course of the ship brought it to within 700 meters of the U20. The time it took the torpedo to get from the bow of the submarine to the ship itself was only forty seconds. Therefore unless a zigzag pattern changed a ship's course every thirty seconds zigzagging would have been of no benefit whatsoever.

So it seems that the advice of the Admiralty to ships entering the danger zone was in many ways of little value to improving the chances of a ship escaping attack and arguably gave the passengers a false sense of security.

In addition to the publicised advice, there was information and instructions given to Captain Turner which were not made public. What were these communication about? It is reasonable to presume that they were militarily sensitive. Why else would Turner refuse to speak of them and declare to the Coroner in Kinsale that he was bound to keep those confidences?

There was no escort provided for RMS *Lusitania* when she entered the exclusion zone. It has been argued that the naval vessels on station were not fast enough to escort the 'greyhound of the seas'; however, the RMS *Lusitania* was operating at a reduced speed because of wartime rationing and even the older warships were comparable. At one point on that fateful morning of 7 May HMS *Juno* was travelling at 16 knots off the south coast of Ireland in a westerly direction while RMS *Lusitania* was travelling at 15 knots having reduced her speed from 18 because of fog. In any event, escorting isn't only about keeping up with a ship. It's about providing a presence in an area, it's about having a deterrent, it's about being on station to assist and protect if the need arises. It is not just about speed.

The action and inactions of HMS *Juno* have still not been satisfactorily explained. There is no doubt that her presence at the site of the sinking of the RMS *Lusitania* would have saved more lives. There is no doubt that HMS *Juno* was just one hour away from hundreds of passengers, injured, traumatised and drowning. There is no doubt that she was armed and capable of inflicting a lethal blow to a submarine. There is no doubt that she was faster than any submarine at the time by a considerable amount. There is no doubt that later in the war slower ships with less weaponry intercepted and sank submarines. Unfortunately there is no doubt that she was ordered back into Cobh where she moored in the safety of the inner harbour, settled there for the night, granted shore leave to sailors on the 'off duty' watch and remained there while other smaller boats far less equipped to deal with rescue or defensive operations went out and braved the sea and its submarines in a humanitarian effort to save lives. The captain of HMS *Juno* and the vice-admiral in Cobh showed a willingness to go to the aid of the victims of the RMS *Lusitania*. The ship and its crew were already on route to put their own lives on the line to save others. The Admiralty recalled them. The log book shows that they turned around and moored to the buoy in Cobh 'as requested'. The question is why was the ship ordered back?

Countless authors have accepted the official line that she was an aging craft, unable to engage with the threat of submarines. As has been outlined already this is not an acceptable or credible answer. A probable and perhaps uncomfortable rationale for the ship to return to port was to increase the loss of life at the scene of the sinking. All other possible reasons have been examined and found improbable. If the motivation of the Admiralty was to increase the loss of life the question must be asked honestly and answered honestly. Was it believed that the loss of as many innocent US civilians as possible would serve to encourage America into the war? If so it may be an understandable position that was taken when the opportunity arose. Perhaps in the belief that the United States would shift the balance of military advances in the overall conflict and save hundreds of thousands or even millions of other lives in the process. But if it was the reason it should be articulated. How many less would have died had the *Juno* gone to the rescue? Captain Turner was in the water for three hours or more and still survived, as did others. HMS *Juno*, had she continued on her course, would have been there an hour before the captain was picked up. Proving that it would have been possible for the *Juno* to save more lives.

The insistence of the Admiralty to divert humanitarian rescue efforts away from Kinsale to Cobh which was another 90 to 120 minutes away defies explanation especially in the case of injured passengers. One author suggests that this was done to prevent any injuries that could be traced to explosives or munitions being seen on any bodies or injured persons from the cargo of the RMS *Lusitania*. It was more likely that it was means by which the Admiralty could control what information emerged. They had tried to prohibit the Coroner in Kinsale from interviewing Captain Turner. The control and release of information by the authorities later certainly helped to colour the narrative afterwards and shape it into the account that it became.

Innocent people died on the RMS *Lusitania* who need not have died. The German Navy, the Cunard shipping company, the customs officials at New York, the Admiralty, the Ministry of Defence in Great Britain and their government all bear some level of responsibility for the sinking of a vessel that wasn't innocent and did not bring the United States into the war.

Notes

Introduction

1   Barbara Tuchman, August 1914 (London, 1962), p.80.
2   *Irish Independent*, 9 May 1914, p.4.

Chapter 1

1   Paul G. Halpern quoting Jellicoe's memoirs in, *A Naval History of World War I* (London, 1994), p.24.

Chapter 2

1   B. Ireland and J. Parker, *The World Encyclopaedia of Destroyers, Frigates and Submarines* (Leicestershire, 2011), p.254.
2   J. Delgado, *Silent Killers: Submarines and Underwater Warfare* (Oxford, 2011), p.19.
3   Ibid., p.52.
4   Ireland and Parker, *Encyclopaedia*, p.254.
5   Delgado, *Silent Killers*, p.258.
6   Ireland and Parker, *Encyclopaedia*, p.260.

7 B. Ireland, *The War at Sea 1914–1945* (London, 2002), p.26.

8 E. Keble & Chatterton, *Danger Zone: The Story of the Queenstown Command* (London, 1934), p.18.

9 Ireland and Parker, *Encyclopaedia*, p.396.

10 Paul G. Halpern, *A Naval History of World War I* (London, 1994), pp7-20.

Chapter 3

1 www.theblueriband.com, accessed 18 January 2014.

2 Mitch Peeke, Kevin Walsh-Johnson and Steve Jones, *The RMS Lusitania Story* (South Yorkshire, 2002), (Electronic edition, 6% Kindle).

3 P. O'Sullivan, *The RMS Lusitania, Unravelling the Mysteries* (Cork, 1998), p.129.

Chapter 4

1 Stuart Robson, *The First World War* (London, 1998), p.1.

2 http://www.firstworldwar.com/origins/causes.htm accessed 12/12/13

3 Robson, *First World War*, p.8.

Chapter 5

1 Ireland and Parker, *Encyclopaedia*, p.128.

2 B. Ireland, *War at Sea 1914-1918*, p.51.

3 E. Keble, Chatterton, *Danger Zone: The Story of the Queenstown Command* (London, 1934), p.45.

4 Paul, G., Halpern, *A Naval History of World War I* (London, 1994), p.26.

5 J., Thompson, *Imperial War Museum Book of the War at Sea 1914-18*, p.629.

Chapter 6

1 J.M., Barry, *Queenstown for Orders*, p.103.
2 Gordon, Campbell, *Rear Admiral, My Mystery Ships* (London, 1928), p.xvi.
3 J., Thompson, *War at Sea 1914-18*, p.632.
4 ibid.
5 Gordon Campbell, *My Mystery Ships* (London, 1928), p.xii.
6 Ibid., p.44.
7 Keble Chatterton, *Danger Zone* (London, 1934), p.122.
8 Ibid., p.126.
9 Patrick Devlin, *Too Proud to Fight, Woodrow Wilson's Neutrality* (London, 1974), p.414.
10 Ibid., p.414.
11 Keble Chatterton, *Danger Zone* (London, 1934), p.89.

Chapter 7

1 Peeke, Jones and Walsh-Johnson, *The RMS Lusitania Story* (Electronic edition, 63% Kindle).
2 Ibid., 64%.

Chapter 8

1 www.RMS Lusitania.net, accessed 12 January 2014.
2 P. O'Sullivan, *The RMS Lusitania, Unravelling the Mysteries* (Cork, 1998), p.89.
3 Bailey and Ryan, *The RMS Lusitania Disaster*, p.165.
4 www.RMS Lusitania.net/hunters accessed 13 January 2014.
5 J., Thompson, *Book of the War at Sea*, p.641
6 Peeke, Jones and Walsh Johnson, *The RMS Lusitania Story* (Electronic edition, 47% Kindle).
7 Julian Thompson, *Imperial War Museum Book of the War at* Sea

1914–18, pp.637-650.

8   P. O'Sullivan, *The RMS Lusitania, Unravelling the Mysteries*, p101.

9   E. Keble, *Chatterton, Danger zone, the story of the Queenstown Command* (London, 1934), p.18.

10 http://oldweather.s3.amazonaws.com/ADM_53-45458/ ADM%2053-45458-006_1.jpg accessed 9 February 2014.

11 Bailey and Ryan, T*he RMS Lusitania Disaster*, p.145.

12 www.naval-history.net/owships-www1-05, accessed January 2014.

13 Peeke, Jones and Walsh Johnson, *The RMS Lusitania Story* (Electronic edition, 30% Kindle).

Chapter 9

1   John Hennessy, interviewed by the author April 2014.

2   K., McCarthy, Essay: 'The Lusitania's Immediate Impact and Lasting Legacy on Cobh' (Queenstown). 21/04/2011.

Chapter 10

1   Keble Chatterton, *Danger Zone, the Story of the Queenstown Command* (London, 1934), p.46.

2   Robert Tucker, *Woodrow Wilson and the Great War, Reconsidering America's Neutrality 1914–1917* (Virginia, 2007).

3   Patrick Devlin, T*oo Proud to Fight, Woodrow Wilson's Neutrality* (London, 1974), p.306.

4   Ernest May, *The Coming of War 1917* (Chicago, 1963), p.49. Quoting Congressional record, 65th Congress, 1st session, pp.102-104.

5   Robert Tucker, *Woodrow Wilson and the Great War* (Virginia, 2007), p.11.

6   Charles Seymour, *American Neutrality 1914-1917: Essays on the Causes of American Intervention in the World War* (Yale University, 1953), p.7.

7   Ernest May, *The Coming of War 1917* (Chicago, 1963), p.4.
    Quoting 'Foreign Relations Supplement: The World War 1915',
    pp.98-99.

8   Ernest May, *The Coming of War*, p.5.

9   Charles Seymour, *American Neutrality*, p5.

10 Paul G. Halpern, *A Naval History of World War I* (London, 1994),
    p.298.

11 Ernest May, *The Coming of War*, p.22.

12 Ibid., p 6, (quoting 'Foreign Relations Supplement: The World
    War, 1915', pp. 393-96.)

13 Ibid.

14 Letter to editor of *The Times Dispatch*, 12 May 1915 by Dr
    Roland Grom in W.H. Tantum (ed), *The RMS Lusitania Case*
    (London, 1972), p.11.

15 W.H. Tantum, *The RMS Lusitania Case*, p.15.

16 Ibid., p.31.

17 Ernest May, *The Coming of War*, p.26 (quoting Foreign
    Relations Supplemen, pp.232-34).

18 Ernest May, *The Coming of War*, p.27.

19 Ibid., p.42.

Chapter 11

1   *New York Times*, 1 May 1915.

Chapter 12

1   Peeke, Jones, Walsh-Johnson, *RMS Lusitania Story*, Foreword by
    Bemis.

2   R. Ballard, *Exploring the RMS Lusitania* (Toronto, 1995), p.147.

3   Chris Reynolds, interviewed by author March 2014.

4   P. O'Sullivan, *The RMS Lusitania, Unravelling the Mysteries*,
    p.137.

5   McGarry interview, 7 March 2104.
6   www.RMS Lusitania.net/hunters, accessed 11 January 2014.
7   Peeke, Jones and Walsh Johnson, *The RMS Lusitania Story* (Electronic edition, 69% Kindle).

Chapter 13

1   A.A. Hoehling and Mary Hoehling, *The Last Voyage of the RMS Lusitania* (New York, 1956), p.39.
2   Cmdr Gene Ryan (retired), interviewed by author January 2014.

Bibliography

Books

Bailey, Thomas A., and Ryan, Paul B., *The Lusitania disaster, an episode in modern warfare and diplomacy* (New York, 1975)

Ballard, Robert D., *Exploring the Lusitania* (Toronto, 1995)

Barry, J.M., *Queenstown for Orders: Queenstown Harbour and the Port of Cork 1800-1922* (Cork, 1999)

Broderick, Mary, *History of Cobh (Queenstown) Ireland* (Cork, 1989)

Broderick, Mary, *RMS Lusitania, the Last Goodbye* (self-published pamphlet Cobh, 2000)

Chatterton, Keble E., *Danger Zone: The Story of the Queenstown Command* (London, 1934)

Delgado, James P., *Silent Killers: Submarines and Underwater Warfare* (Oxford, 2011)

Devlin, Patrick, *Too Proud to Fight, Woodrow Wilson's Neutrality* (London, 1974)

Halpern, Paul G., *A Naval History of World War I* (London, 1994)

Hochschild, Adam, *To End All Wars: How the First World War Divided Britain* (London, 2013)

Horgan, John J., *Parnell to Pearse* (Dublin, 1949)

Ireland, Bernard, *War at Sea 1914–45* (London, 2002)

Ireland, Bernard and Parker, John, *The World Encyclopaedia of*

Destroyers, Frigates & Submarines (Leicestershire, 2011)

Jeffery, Keith, *Ireland and the Great War* (Cambridge, 2000)

Jones, Steve, Walsh-Johnson, Kevin and Peeke, Mitch, *The Lusitania Story* (2002)

Liddle, Peter, *The Sailor's War 1914–18* (Dorset, 1985)

Malony, Senan, *Lusitania: An Irish Tragedy* (Dublin, 2004)

May, Ernest, R., *The Coming of War, 1917* (Chicago, 1963). From the Berkeley Series in American History ed. Charles Sellers.

O'Sullivan, Patrick, *The Lusitania: Unravelling the Mysteries* (Cork, 1998)

Ramsay, David, *Lusitania: Saga and Myth* (Kent, 2001)

Robson, Stuart, *The First World War* (London, 1998)

Seymour, Charles, *American Neutrality 1914–1917: Essays on the Causes of Intervention in the World War* (Yale University, 1935)

Self, Robert, *Britain, America and the war debt controversy, the economic diplomacy of an unspecial relationship, 1914–1941* (Oxon, 2006)

Simpson, Colin, *Lusitania* (London, 1972)

Smith, F.A., Thomas, *What Germany thinks* (London, 1915)

Strachan, Hew, *Financing the First World War* (Oxford, 2004)

Tantum IV, W.H., (ed.), *The Lusitania Case: Documents on the War* (London, 1972), first published in 1916 and collected by C.L. Droste.

Thompson, Julian, *Imperial War Museum Book of the War at Sea 1914–18* (Pan ebook, 2011)

Tuchman, Barbara, *August 1914* (London, 1962)

Tucker, Robert, W., *Woodrow Wilson and the Great War, reconsidering America's neutrality 1914–1917* (Virginia, 2007)

Websites

www.lusitania.net

Index

Also from The History Press

Irish
Revolutionaries

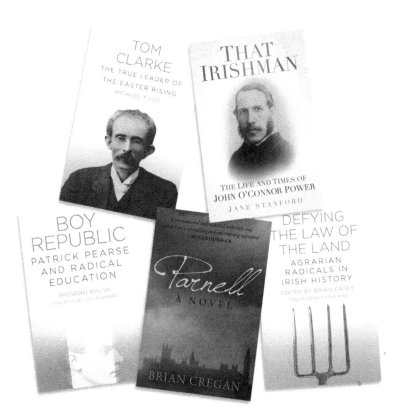

Also from The History Press

Irish
Women

Find these titles and more at
www.thehistorypress.ie